TOWARDS THE SETTING SUN

TOWARDS
the
SETTING SUN

An escape from the
Thailand~Burma Railway, 1943

James Bradley

Jim Bradley

23. 8. 85.

1984
Published by
J. M. L. FULLER
10 Jean Street
Wellington N.S.W.

First edition 1982

ISBN 0 9590187 0 0

Printed at Griffin Press Limited
Marion Road, Netley, South Australia 5037

CONTENTS

ARREST AND TRIAL

EPILOGUE

APPENDICES

LIST OF MAPS

LIST OF PHOTOGRAPHS

(between pages 44 and 45)

1. The Author, James Bradley, 1940
2. Lindsay and Roger, 1940
3. The Surrender, 15 February 1942
4. Roberts Barracks before hostilities
5. Photograph of Lindsay and Roger, received at Changi
6. Two bridges at Tha Makham
7. Hintok Bridge, 1945
8. The Three Pagodas
9. C5631 locomotive in opening ceremony of Thailand/ Burma railway, 1943
10. C5631 locomotive at Yasukuni Shrine, Tokyo, 1979
11. Changi Gaol, 1980
12. Photograph of Roger and Penny Knowles, received in Changi Gaol, December 1943
13. The grave of Col. C. H. D. Wild, M.B.E.
14. Jim, Lindy, Timothy and Sarah, October 1981

For my family,
and for the families of all those
who did not return

ACKNOWLEDGMENTS

Special Acknowledgment
I would like to thank Geoffrey Pharaoh Adams, R.A.S.C. and
ex-FEPOW, author of *No Time for Geishas, The Thailand to
Burma Railway* and *Destination Japan*, for his invaluable
enthusiasm and encouragement, without which this book
could never have appeared in its present form. No-one could
have been more kind or generous in his offer of help, with his
unique private collection of documents, letters and photographs. He must be one of the greatest authorities on the
Thailand/Burma Railway, and even now he seems to hear
daily of new discoveries about the Railway, and the proposed
flooding of the Sonkurai area after a hydro-electric dam has
been built.

Special Acknowledgment
I would like to thank Capt. C. Ewart Escritt, OBE, R.A.S.C.,
and ex-FEPOW, for allowing me to use three short quotes
from his notes of May 1981, entitled *A Japanese Railway
Engineer's Trace of the Thailand–Burma Rail Link Line in
the Imperial War Museum, London*. These appear in Chapter 5.

I am enormously grateful to Capt. Escritt for the trouble
he has taken and the time he has spent on the accuracy and
general construction of this book, and also for writing the
short review of my story, which appears on the front flap of
the dust-cover. He is also a great authority on World War 2
in the Far East.

* * *

I have quoted from *Narrative of 'F' Force in Thailand, April
1943–December 1943*, by Capt. Cyril H. D. Wild (Ox. and

Bucks. L.I.). (G. P. Adams Private Collection, and by kind permission of The Very Revd. J. H. S. Wild, MA.)

I would like to thank The Very Revd. J. H. S. Wild, MA, for allowing me to quote his late brother's poem, *Sonkurai Labour Camp.*

* * *

I have quoted and used certain information from *Report on POWs in Thailand, May to December 1943*, by Lt.-Col. F. J. Dillon, OBE, MC (AA & QMG, 18th Div.). (G. P. Adams Private Collection.)

* * *

I have quoted and used certain information from the Official Medical Reports, 1942–1945, POW Camp, Changi. (G. P. Adams Private Collection.)

* * *

After the Battle Magazine, issue nos. 26 and 31 have been helpful to me. (Editor: Winston G. Ramsey.)

* * *

I would like to thank H. M. Burkill and L. J. Robertson for some extremely interesting items of information which I have been able to put into this revised edition.

* * *

I would like to thank Professor T. Wilson for allowing me to quote from his diary.

* * *

I would like to thank Eric Lomax for the information he has given me concerning his party of fellow prisoners who were arrested for operating a secret radio, and also for his personal knowledge of 'Operation Rimau'.

I would also like to thank Eric for forgiving me for his early demise in the first edition! The renewal of our friendship is a wonderful result of writing this book.

* * *

Since the first edition was published I have discovered that Ian Moffat, one of my fellow escapees, is alive and well in Argentina. To him and to all those who have written to me, many with extremely interesting reminders, I would like to offer my thanks. Those letters make the whole effort of writing this book so worthwhile.

SONKURAI LABOUR CAMP

(Thailand Railway 1943)

Qui ante diem perierunt

At Sonkurai, where hope lay drowned
Beneath the bridge, the earth is browned
   With mould, sad monsoon-vapours veil
   The jungle, and the creepers trail
Like snakes inert, their coils unwound.

And there our rear-guard keep their ground
(Eight comrades laid beneath each mound),
   A thousand, dead without avail,
      At Sonkurai.

Freed from the captive's weary round,
Homeless, a lasting home they found.
   Let not our faith their courage fail,
   Till with the dawn the stars turn pale
And (silent long) our bugles sound
      At Sonkurai!

CYRIL WILD

Singapore, June 1944

FOREWORD

This is the true account of how my husband, Jim, together
with nine others, attempted an incredible escape from
Sonkurai, one of the most northern jungle camps in Thailand
on the Burma–Thailand railway. Out of the ten original
members who started to hack their way through previously
unpenetrated dense jungle, only five survived, and these five
were cruelly betrayed and sold back to the Japanese. There
then followed months of deprivation, almost beyond human
endurance, although why they weren't shot or bayoneted to
death immediately upon recapture, the fate that befell all
other escapees, remains a mystery; unless the Japanese were
so impressed by what they had achieved. For five under-
nourished and sick men to survive eight weeks in the jungle,
living on water only for the last three weeks, was no mean
feat. Special gratitude must be due to Capt. (later Col.) Cyril
Wild, MBE, who had gone to witness their execution and was
able to persuade Col. Banno of the shame he would bring on
the Emperor and the Imperial Japanese Army by executing
these brave men.

Jim, who was a Sapper, saw 30 days of action in Singapore
before it fell to the Japanese. He then spent 14 months in
Changi POW Camp before being made to march for three
hundred kilometres, as a member of the 'ill-fated' 'F' Force,
from Ban Pong to the very top of the Thailand section of the
infamous railway that the Japanese were building, with POW
forced labour, so that they could transport troops and
supplies to Burma, in preparation for their invasion of India.
The conditions under which they were made to work were
unimaginable, and the combined effects of overwork, malnutrition, starvation and disease drastically reduced their

numbers in a very short time. There were few survivors from Sonkurai, compared with the numbers that went up there, and certainly no survivors of other escapes in South East Asia, and therefore this account is of a unique experience. For this reason, I believe Jim's book has an empty place to fill in the archives of contemporary history.

The escape was deemed necessary by those ten men, led by Col. Mike Wilkinson, to bring to the notice of the International Red Cross the frightful treatment the Allied prisoners of the Japanese were being forced to endure. The rest of the world had been told that the Japanese treated their POWs well; only the POWs themselves knew differently. Their reason for escape was not desertion—a charge upon which the Japanese kept insisting at their subsequent trial by Military Court Martial at Raffles College in Singapore.

In 1945 Lady Louis Mountbatten asked Jim to write a book about the escape, but out of respect for the feelings of the widows and families of those who had died such terrible deaths, he would not do it at that time. However, now that 36 years have elapsed, he has decided to do it, and indeed, writing the book has been a wonderful therapy for him. Ever since he returned home in 1945 he has been unable to speak of his appalling experiences, and it has all been 'bottled up' inside him, plaguing him relentlessly with nightmares. All he wanted to do was try and forget, and it took a great deal of persuasion on my part to convince him that his remarkable story should be recorded for posterity. Bringing the memories to the forefront of his mind was an ordeal for him, but now that it is done, he feels that a great weight has been lifted from his shoulders.

By March 1981, the original manuscript was completed. Characteristically, Jim had not wanted to write a horror story, but a human and feeling book, containing much of his personal life and family history. He wrote it for his family, entirely from memory and with no thoughts of it being published. However, we subsequently received so much encouragement from the many people who read it, especially Geoffrey Pharaoh Adams, whose book, *No Time for Geishas*, really inspired us, that we felt we should do a re-write, with publication in mind, and this is the result. We have now done some research and gone into more detail, though at the same time we were determined that it should remain a human and feeling story.

Other books have been written, giving many statistics, facts and figures of this particular area of World War 2. Jim does not attempt to reiterate all these, but simply to write about his own experiences, impressions and thoughts, and by so doing he takes the welcome opportunity to acknowledge, with deep gratitude, the utter unselfishness of certain people he knew in his POW days. People's best characteristics are always most evident in times of real stress. One of Jim's is always to look on the bright side, and this shows in the book, even in the most desperate situations; nowhere does the word 'despair' occur. Jim never despaired, and he never gave up hope.

For Jim there is no mental escape. However, he bears no malice towards the Japanese people, insisting that one must look to the future with friendship and mutual understanding, and learn from the mistakes of the past. The young Japanese people of today must not feel guilty, nor must they take the blame for the actions of their fathers and grandfathers, and of course, it must be remembered that, traditionally, their sense of values was so different from our own. At the time of the Second World War they still felt that it was honourable to fight to the death and die in battle, and that it was a humiliating disgrace to be taken prisoner and held in captivity.

After the Japanese surrender in 1945 thousands of Japanese POWs are alleged to have committed suicide, and I think they were amazed that the Allied POWs had not done the same thing in 1942; they were overwhelmed by the numbers of men suddenly in their hands, and realized at once what a vast source of labour they had at their disposal. They treated

---

Since writing *Towards the Setting Sun* we have learnt that there was, in fact, a successful escape from the railway. Private Pagani, a Eurasian of 18th Division Recce Corps, and ultimately a member of the Sumatra/British Battalion under Capt. Dudley Apthorp, Royal Norfolks, escaped from a camp 18 kms. south of Thanbyuzayat shortly after arriving in Burma in November 1942. His skin colour no doubt helped him to elude capture, and he took refuge in a convent in Tavoy until he returned to the U.K., via India, in June 1945.

Towards the Setting Sun

their prisoners with contempt, and never ratified the Geneva Convention for POWs. Taking into account this difference in traditional values, this book is not, therefore, a criticism and no offence is intended; but it must never happen again.

The actual fighting prior to the fall of Singapore is dealt with only briefly, as we have made no attempt to examine army records and in any case it has all been written before.

The following pages tell of enormous courage, endurance and determination: determination to survive and come home to a wife and young son. It does not make light bedtime reading. There are other numerous war stories of real heroism, courage, tragedy, suffering and glory. In Jim's war there was no glory.

LINDY BRADLEY

September, 1981

PROLOGUE

Chapter 1

EARLY DAYS

IT WAS the late summer of 1938, and my mother had rented a large house in Abersoch for what turned out to be the last holiday we were to enjoy as a complete family.

My elder brother was there with his wife and small son, but it was at the time of the Munich Crisis and Jock was recalled to his Territorial Unit. I was there with my wife, Lindsay, and Roger who was just over one month old, together with my younger sister, Beth.

Jock's call-up and the general international situation put a dampener on the remainder of the holiday, and on my return home to Deganwy I joined a newly-formed Territorial Regiment of Anti-Aircraft Gunners at Chester, as I felt war was then inevitable.

War came almost a year later, but I had been mobilized ten days earlier. I remained with the Unit for some time, and was posted to an R.E. OCTU in Aldershot as I had a Cambridge Engineering Degree. Just before the end of the six months' course I was commissioned early as a Full Lieutenant and retained at the OCTU as a Class Officer. After taking one class through their course I asked to be released, and was posted to 18th Division, R.E. This Division was basically an East Anglian Territorial Formation, comprising the Norfolk, Suffolk and Cambridgeshire Regiments and their ancillary forces. They were commanded by a Welsh Guardsman, Major General M. B. Beckwith-Smith, who, sadly, died early during his captivity in Formosa (Taiwan).

Incredibly, I also received a second posting, with an entirely different army number, which complicated my pay in no uncertain terms! It was not until I received a small award after the war that my correct army number was established.

1

I duly reported to the C.R.E. at Knutsford in Cheshire in May 1941, and was posted to 287 Field Company, R.E., in Liverpool. Our Company was billeted on Lord Sefton's estate at Croxteth, as we were helping during the Liverpool bombing, and it was here that I met, for the first time, Major M. T. L. Wilkinson (later Lt.-Col.), my Company Commander. He was a regular officer, and one of the finest characters I have ever known.

Mike was totally unselfish and at all times had the interests of his men at heart. Later, as a prisoner, he would accept nothing that might have made life a little easier that his men could not share. He was a big man in every way, and at 19 stone had played rugger for the Sappers, and even hurdled for them, although he claimed any hurdle he hit had to be replaced! Affectionately known by everyone as 'Wilkie', he had a wonderful sense of humour which never left him, even in our darkest times, and I consider myself fortunate to have served under him. I valued his friendship at that time above all else.

We were given a few days' embarkation leave, and on my return to Liverpool I took our transport and equipment to Port Sunlight for shipment. We then left by train from Aintree Station for the Clyde, and boarded the *Duchess of Atholl* at Greenock.

Chapter 2

TROOPING

(i) To Halifax, Nova Scotia

WITHIN THE NEXT few days the whole Division had embarked, part in Liverpool, part at Avonmouth and part at Greenock. We set sail on 27th October 1941, escorted by a single British Naval Cruiser, H.M.S. *Calypso*, having no idea of our ultimate destination, but equipped with tropical gear. The rumour that appeared to be the most informed was that we were heading for the Persian Gulf, with the object of linking up with the Russians in the Caucasus.

As we sailed down the Clyde I stood on deck, watching the land slip by, and later the Isles of Bute and Arran. My thoughts were in a turmoil. This was a big step into the unknown, as we had no definite idea of our destination or for how long we were leaving our native country. In war there must always be the question of whether or not we would be the lucky ones to return to our families.

I thought back over my life and realised how lucky I had been, having had a secure and happy childhood with my elder brother and younger sister, and with wonderful parents, who I think must have made sacrifices to give us, what I believe, was a good sound education. Jock and I went to a preparatory school in North Wales, where during my last year Evelyn Waugh came as an assistant master. We both went on to Oundle and Christ's College, Cambridge. My father had died young, having been badly gassed in the First World War, but we were a united and happy family, and this I shall never forget.

And now, as we crept away from England, I was leaving Lindsay and Roger, who were my whole world, and there on the deck of the *Duchess of Atholl* I prayed that we would be reunited in the not too distant future. As dusk fell, I went below to join the others for a good strong drink, to help me snap out of this mood of apprehension.

Our ship, like her sister ship, the *Duchess of Richmond*, had always carried the nickname of 'The Drunken Duchess', because of her rolling habits, but I am sure we fared no worse than the other ships in our convoy in the heavy seas we were to meet. We had most comfortable cabins with no overcrowding, and we probably travelled in as much comfort as would have been possible in pre-war days.

Drink was plentiful and cheap, and we were young. The catering was of an extremely high standard, as the ships had been revictualled in South Africa, and we had an endless choice of courses at each meal, something we really appreciated having come from rationing at home. The men were also well fed, and this was the one topic they mentioned in their letters home, so the censoring of letters became almost a formality, for which I was very glad. It always seemed an invasion of the men's privacy to read their personal letters, but I suppose in some cases it could be necessary; as far as I remember, I had to eliminate very little, and that was not until we had reached Singapore.

The amount of training that can be carried out while at sea is necessarily very limited, and with no equipment aboard, was confined to theory. It was intended to hold lectures and talks during the morning training sessions, but even these had to be abandoned almost immediately, owing to the very rough weather.

After about a week the American Navy took over, and we had a particularly strong escort under Rear Admiral H. K. Hewitt, U.S.N., comprising one aircraft carrier, two heavy cruisers, and nine modern destroyers, with the planes from the carrier searching a wide area around us for any sign of German U-boats or Italian submarines. Some of these same planes flew low over the convoy, dropping messages of welcome on each ship. After a fairly rough crossing, we entered the calm, still waters of Halifax, Nova Scotia, where we transferred into American troop ships, although America was not yet in the war.

In 1944 I was to learn from an Italian submarine comman-der, who came into the POW camp at Changi when the Italians ceased hostilities, that he had shadowed us during the early stages of our Atlantic crossing, and I am convinced that this was true, as he could name all the ships in our convoy. Luckily for us he had been unwilling to waste torpedoes, because of the heavy seas, and he left us alone when we were taken over by the American fleet, as we were then so heavily escorted.

To one coming from a country which was blacked out, the lights of Halifax were a wonderful sight, and those who wished went ashore for the evening.

On leaving Halifax on 10th November 1941, the convoy was under the command of Rear Admiral A. B. Cook, U.S. Navy, and comprised:

U.S.S. *Mount Vernon*	(ex S.S. *Washington*)
U.S.S. *Wakefield*	(ex S.S. *Manhattan*)
U.S.S. *Westpoint*	(ex S.S. *America*, the flagship of the U.S. Merchant Navy, and only recently commissioned)
U.S.S. *Leonard Wood*	(ex S.S. *Western World*, Munson Line)
U.S.S. *Joseph Dickman*	(ex Munson Line)
U.S.S. *Orizaba*	(ex Ward Line)

The escort itself comprised U.S.S. *Ranger*, a fleet aircraft carrier, supported by two heavy cruisers, U.S.S. *Vincennes* and U.S.S. *Quincy*, and eight modern destroyers under the command of Captain T. C. Kinkaid, U.S.N. He and his flotilla left the convoy at Port of Spain, and he was later to lead the mighty U.S. Seventh Fleet in the victorious battles to the shores of Japan.

(ii) To Mombasa and Singapore

We, in the 53rd Brigade, transferred to the *Mount Vernon*, in which we had even more spacious accommodation but, unfor-tunately, these troop ships came under the American Navy and were thus dry. This hit us badly after our cheap drink on the transatlantic crossing, and the food was nothing like as good as that on the first part of our journey, there being little variety.

During the whole time we were trooping we had to keep our life-jackets to hand, and attached to mine I always had a small brandy flask and my travellers cheques. My line of thought was that the brandy might help me to overcome the rigours of being torpedoed, and if I eventually landed anywhere, a little money would certainly not come amiss. Contraceptive sheaths were part of a Sapper's standard equipment for keeping detonators dry, and it was in one of these that I kept my cheques.

After leaving Halifax we headed south, but the three smaller vessels slowed down the convoy considerably, as they had a very poor turn of speed. We passed through some very heavy weather off Cape Hatteras, but later sailed into calmer seas.

We were now entering the tropics, and the weather was getting really warm, with unbroken sunshine, though there was a constant breeze due to the passage of our ship. We changed into tropical gear, and with this sudden improvement in the weather there seemed to be a completely new spirit aboard, and thus we came to Trinidad and dropped anchor in the clear waters of the Caribbean, about five miles off Port of Spain. Here we remained for about a week, lapping up the sunshine, but unfortunately there was no shore leave, probably because of the difficulty of getting so many people ashore by lighter. However, a lucky few landed to buy supplies for a canteen.

At Trinidad we were joined by the fleet tanker, U.S.S. *Cimarron*, and as we crossed the Southern Atlantic we were to see this tanker refuelling the smaller ships of our convoy. At this point we still believed that our destination was Basra. Naval intelligence gave warning of a likely heavy U-boat attack, and the convoy therefore sailed south and into the 'Roaring Forties'.

Several days out from Cape Town, on 7th December 1941, the Japanese launched their devastating attack on Pearl Harbour, and thus brought our hosts firmly into the war. On the day we entered Cape Town, 10th December 1941, we heard of the tragic loss of H.M.S. *Repulse* and H.M.S. *Prince of Wales*. This gave us plenty of food for thought, and we felt almost certain that we should now be destined for Singapore. We lay off Cape Town for what seemed a ridiculously long time, while it was decided whether General Beckwith-Smith, commanding 18th Division, or the American Commodore should take precedence and enter Cape Town first.

The people of Cape Town must be the most hospitable in the world, as they put themselves out to look after everyone in the convoy, and were waiting in their hundreds to welcome us all; nothing was too much trouble, nor did they spare any expense. They were proud of their country and their homes, which they delighted in sharing with us all. Ours was one of the early convoys into Cape Town, and certainly the first time the American Navy had visited there during the war. The population really put themselves out, organizing receptions and dances, the main ball being at Kelvin Grove Country Club where Field-Marshal Smuts was guest of honour.

I was most impressed with the part of South Africa I saw, and so enjoyed my time there that I really felt I would love to bring Lindsay and Roger and make our home there after the war. The only flaws, in what otherwise seemed perfection, were the colour segregation notices. It has always been a failing of mine to be carried away by the beauty of new places, and when I returned home after the war, naturally I was restless, and very seriously considered farming in Kenya. Thank goodness Lindsay understood the temporary nature of my wanderlust and kept my feet firmly on the ground.

After our idyllic time in South Africa, we put to sea again, with changed orders for Bombay, H.M.S. *Dorsetshire* being our sole escort and her single Walrus Amphibian our lone look-out, whilst the American ships returned to their home bases for deployment elsewhere.

The *Mount Vernon* carried a complete Brigade, the 53rd, commanded by Brigadier C. L. B. Duke, CB, MC, late R.E., known to all as 'Bulger' Duke. Before reaching Bombay we dropped off the convoy and returned to Kilindini, the port of Mombasa, where we remained for Christmas week. It was most impressive entering the harbour, as the deep water channel ran close to the land and parallel to it, and we were almost looking down from the deck onto the golf course. We were told that, at the time, we were the largest ship to date ever to have tied up alongside in the harbour.

Mombasa was a comparatively small town in those days, so there was obviously very little in the way of organized hospitality for the troops. Here, as in Cape Town, we normally went for route marches in the mornings, and on one march we passed a small POW camp, housing Italian prisoners, but they appeared to be well accommodated and looked happy and fit. We all badly needed these route marches, because of the lack of exercise on the troop ships. We had already been trooping for two months.

Several of us went up to a beach, just north of Mombasa, where the bathing was superb. I think this must have been Nyali Beach, which at that time was merely a long stretch of sand backed by a fringe of palm trees, whereas now, of course, it has been developed in the same way as White Sands and Malindi, and must have lost most of its natural charm. However, I would still love to return there with my family for a holiday!

On leaving harbour, we headed for an atoll in the Indian Ocean, where we joined up with another convoy, including H.M.S. *Ajax* and H.M.S. *Exeter*, still bearing their battle scars from the River Plate action, and the Dutch cruiser, *De Ruyter*. We then headed south of east across the Indian Ocean until we reached the Sunda Straits, between Sumatra and Java.

We passed near the site of the extinct volcano, Krakatoa, before sailing through the Straits and eventually into the Naval Base at Singapore on 13th January 1942, unmolested by enemy bombers due to bad visibility. It was two days after my sixth wedding anniversary. We had been trooping for just over eleven weeks, and had it not been for the uncertainty of events, and the fact that I was leaving Lindsay and Roger, I should have enjoyed it all.

The other two Brigades of 18th Division, the 54th and 55th, had duly arrived and disembarked at Bombay. However, at a later date they re-embarked and were taken to Singapore very shortly before the surrender, and in my opinion, though I am probably quite wrong, their presence in this theatre of war could have achieved nothing. Singapore was already virtually lost, and I still feel they were sent in as a sacrificial token.

Sadly, the *Exeter* and the *De Ruyter* were lost after leaving Singapore, in the battle of the Java Sea.

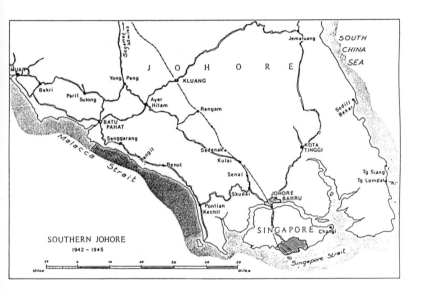

Map 1. Southern Malaya

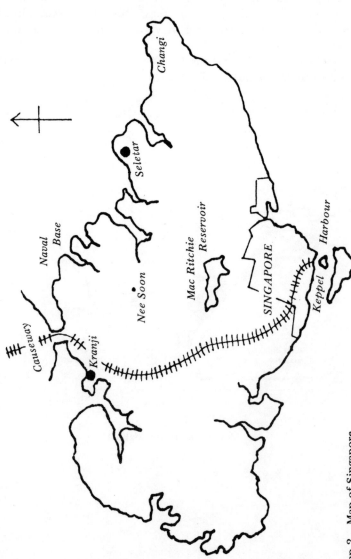

Map 2.   Map of Singapore

Chapter 3
CAMPAIGN AND SURRENDER

AFTER DISEMBARKING at the Naval Base, on the north shore of Singapore Island, we joined a unit which had been stationed on the Island for some time, where we were received very hospitably and made guests of their officers' mess. As we had only just arrived in the country, an officer from the Straits Settlement Volunteer Force, Capt. A. Hay, and a younger officer from the Federated Malay States Volunteer Force, H. M. Burkill, were attached to us for liaison. Their knowledge of the country, the people and the language was a great help to us, and without them we would have been completely lost.

We were given an official printed document, telling us how to differentiate between Japanese, Chinese and Malays. The one significant difference, we were told, was that the Japanese always walked with their toes turned in, but this was very little help when they were driving a truck or a tank, or even riding a bicycle! We were later to see that they had their own particular style of cycling, and this was to put their heels on the pedals, with their toes turned outwards!

This rather useless document also gave us particulars of how payment would be made to the families and dependents of prisoners of war, should Singapore fall; not a particularly encouraging start to our service overseas! Also, we were each issued with a collar stud, in which there was a hidden compass, with instructions to scrape off the backing if the time came when we should need to make use of it for the purpose of escaping.

We spent a fairly hectic 48 hours here, re-equipping ourselves with the necessary Sapper technical gear, and with the normal transport for the Company. Our own transport had

11

gone on to India with the remainder of our original convoy, and most of it was eventually lost before reaching Singapore.

With practically no acclimatization period, we were sent into action on the mainland, not really knowing the difference between the Eastern races; they all looked much alike to us. Never had such a raw and untried group of men gone into action! We had few large-scale maps of the area, and were completely untrained in jungle warfare. We moved up to Ayer Hitam in Johore, where we established our Company Headquarters; the front, at this time, was roughly between Malacca on the west and Mersing on the east.

I went out on detachment with my Section to prepare demolitions along the Yong Peng to Muar road, and we took over a wooden house, standing on stilts, that had already been evacuated. Except for a python! On looking round our new billet, we found this tremendous snake, coiled up underneath the house, but we did not disturb him and he didn't worry about us, remaining almost immobile for the few days we were there.

The road to the west of Yong Peng was, in fact, a causeway over marshy land, and it was in this part of the road that we blew camouflets and laid charges to blow craters, hoping to stop enemy vehicles. I had, of course, to leave a few men in charge of each demolition we had prepared, and when visiting them during the night I left a bottle of whisky with each group to help keep up their morale, as these were lonely spots in which to be left in a completely new country. Until that night, none of us had ever seen fireflies in such numbers, and the bushes surrounding us seemed to be afire with them. When drawing equipment from the Naval Base on arrival, I had been given a couple of cases of whisky, which I carried in my truck, and very useful they proved to be.

The Army had been steadily retreating down the mainland, and before making yet another withdrawal, I received orders from Brigade, through my Company Headquarters, to take over the responsibility of the bridge at Muar, which had been prepared for demolition by the Australians. I went out, with both my sergeant, C. E. Pilgrim, and my driver, T. H. Hotson, in my Ford V8 truck, to make a reconnaissance, and I contacted the Australian detachment at the bridge. The officer in charge showed me his written orders, that on no account were they to blow the bridge or hand over responsibility to anyone else, as many of their troops were still north of this point; their only means of withdrawal was across this one bridge. I had no option but to return and report this to my Company Commander.

However, while I was at Muar, a Japanese patrol had come round behind us and had ambushed and killed three dispatch riders, leaving them obstructing the road, together with their machines. As I had been unable to take over responsibility of the bridge, it was vital that I should get back to make my report, as then we had no radio contact, so we made a dash for it over the cycles, and were very lucky not to have been killed, as the patrol opened fire. Although my truck was holed in several places, we managed to get through, but it was a close thing, as I got a graze on my shoulder and lost one of my pips!

On approaching Yong Peng, I was signalled to stop by an officer of either the 5th or 6th Royal Norfolk Regiment, and taken to make my report direct to General Percival and General Heath, who had come forward to Yong Peng at the time. This I did, and gave them details of the position at Muar. Later, the Indians suffered a terrible massacre at that village.

After withdrawing to Pontian Kechil, where the Company reformed, we moved to Senggarang, where we were all billeted together in an old school for the night. It was from Senggarang that an ill-fated column left to try and open up the road south of Batu Pahat, where many of 5th and 6th Royal Norfolk Regiment were cut off. The column suffered heavy losses and failed to get through, and the majority of the beleaguered troops at Batu Pahat were taken prisoner and ended up in Changi. Before withdrawing south we finally blew the road bridge at Senggarang. It seems to have been a very successful demolition as not only did the complete span drop but the abutments and foundations were shattered. It was not until 1966 that the bridge was rebuilt by the Public Works Department.

We had no tanks and very few tracked vehicles of any

description, apart from a limited number of Bren gun carriers, and the only British planes we ever saw were a few Brewster Buffaloes and one Tiger Moth. Forty crated Hurricanes were landed in Singapore from our convoy, but these had to be assembled and some were damaged on the ground before they had ever flown. By 9th February only six Hurricanes remained airworthy after hundreds of Japanese dive bombers had attacked the defences and airfields. The Japanese had complete air superiority, and formations of heavy bombers came over, releasing all their bombs simultaneously; this we came to know as 'pattern bombing'. The dive bombers, together with their Zero Fighters, had no opposition.

From Senggarang we made our final withdrawal from the mainland, over the 1100 yard long Causeway and on to Singapore Island. One of my first jobs on the Island was to blow up the jetty and waterfront installations, including a crane, at Seletar Aerodrome, which by now had been evacuated by most of the RAF personnel. This was part of an overall policy to leave nothing serviceable for the enemy. I saw the remaining senior officer to inform him of my instructions, and he told me that the pier carried the main fuel pipeline, assuring me, however, that all valves had been turned off. Nevertheless, when I finally blew the installation, there was no lack of fuel in the pipes, and it caused a tremendous blaze which could be seen all over the Island.

Our Company finally assumed an Infantry role and took up positions near the MacRitchie Reservoir, in the central part of the Island, as this should be held at all costs. The main water supply for Singapore Island came from the mainland in Johore, and since the Japanese were now in full control of the mainland, they only had to turn off the water supply for the Island to deprive the whole of the civilian population, as well as the Army, of water, except for the small amount available from this reservoir. The importance of this can be appreciated, as it was one of the main reasons for what seemed to be an early surrender of all Allied Forces.

This is shown in the following Order of the Day, signed by Lt.-Gen. Percival:

'It has been necessary to give up the struggle and I want

the reason explained to all ranks. The forward troops
continue to hold their ground, but the essentials of war
have run short. In a few days we shall have neither petrol
nor food. Many types of ammunition have run short,
and the water supply, on which the vast civilian population and many of the fighting troops are dependent,
threatens to fail. This situation has been brought about,
partly by being driven off our dumps and partly by
hostile air attack and artillery action. Without these
sinews of war we cannot carry on.

I thank all ranks for their efforts during the campaign.

(Signed) A. E. Percival
Lt.-Gen.'

Later, I was given a copy of the letter from Lt.-Gen.
Tomoyuki Yamashita, High Commander of the Nippon 25th
Army in Malaya, calling upon the Commander of the British
Army to surrender:

'To the High Commander of the British Army in Malaya,
Feb. 10th 2602

Your Excellency,

I, the Commander of the Nippon Army in Malaya,
based on the spirit of Japan's chivalry, have the honour
of presenting this note to your Excellency, advising you
to surrender the whole forces in Malaya. My sincere
respect is due to your army, which, true to the traditional spirit of Great Britain, is defending Singapore, which
now stands isolated, and unaided. Many fierce and fear-
less fights have been fought by your gallant men and
officers, to the honour and glory of British warriorship.
But the development of the general war situation has
sealed the fate of Singapore and the continuation of
futile resistance would only serve to inflict direct harm
and injuries to thousands of non-combatants living in
the city, and would certainly not add anything to the
honour of your army. I expect that your Excellency will
accept my advice, will give up this meaningless and

desperate resistance and promptly order the entire front to cease hostilities and will despatch at the same time your parliamentaire, according to the procedure shown at the end of this note. If, on the contrary, your Excellency should reject my advice, and the present resistance be continued I shall be advised, though reluctantly, from humanitarian consideration to order my army to make annihilating attacks on Singapore. In closing this note, I pay my respects to your Excellency.

(Signed) Lt.-Gen. Tomoyuki Yamashita
High Commander of the Nippon Army in Malaya

N.B. The parliamentaire shall bear a large white flag and the Union Jack. The parliamentaire shall proceed along Bukit Timah Road.'

General Percival, accompanied by three staff officers, duly met General Yamashita at the Ford Motor Company factory at Bukit Timah, at 4.30 p.m. on 15th February 1942. Capt. C. H. D. Wild carried the white flag, and acted as interpreter. At 7.50 p.m. General Percival signed the surrender, and just over two hours later the fighting stopped.

Our position, near the MacRitchie Reservoir, was the first and only one where we actually dug slit trenches, being under fairly consistent mortar fire. It was here, on 15th February, that Capt. C. D. Pickersgill, Mike Wilkinson's second in command, came to notify us that Singapore had surrendered, and to give us a point at which to rendezvous. We formed up with the remainder of the Company, and marched down into Singapore to one of the assembly points, where we had to lay down our arms. It was a sad and degrading moment.

We were instructed that no officers would attempt to escape, as one of the conditions of terms of surrender was that officers would not be segregated and would remain in charge of their men. At this time, there would have been a reasonable chance of getting away, had one been allowed to do so, as many small vessels were lying in Singapore Harbour, and several were making for Sumatra.

Obviously, we were not allowed to leave the house allocated to us, which was situated on a cross-roads, where two or three Japanese troops were posted. It was from an upper window in this house that I saw one of these Japanese shoot, in cold blood, a passer-by (either a Chinese or a Malay), because he did not appear to have understood an order. His body lay at the side of the road, until two more locals approached and were made to scrape the dust from the side of the road with their bare hands, to cover the unfortunate victim.

On 16th February the order to move to Changi was given, and so we formed up with other units and started our march to the north-east coast of the Island, a distance of 17 miles. We were all carrying as much as we could in the way of spare clothing, blankets, canned food, and in fact anything which might prove useful, and those who still had their camp beds and mosquito nets carried these as well. I was one of those fortunate enough to have kept mine, as it had been in my personal truck all the time.

Many of the inhabitants of Singapore had already obtained Japanese flags, which they were displaying from their windows, but apart from some of the more horrible remains of fighting, the journey was like any other route march in that we were completely unescorted.

The defeat at Singapore had caused the Allies the loss of nearly 140,000 Australian, British and Indian troops killed, wounded or captured, compared with 9,824 Japanese casualties. In the course of the next few days all the Allied troops had assembled at Changi, as prisoners of war, and we in the 53rd Brigade had seen just 30 days of action.

Chapter 4

CHANGI

(i) POW in Changi

CHANGI POW CAMP had originally been a large British military base, and had been evacuated on 7th February 1942. It was in the north-eastern corner of Singapore Island, bounded on the north by the Johore Straits and on the east and south-east by the sea. The ground within the Area was undulating and well wooded, with coconut and rubber predominating. Much of the swampy foreshore was covered with mangrove, and everywhere there was lalang grass.

There was a heavy annual rainfall, with no actual dry season, but at two periods throughout the year, March to May and October to November, rainfall was heaviest. Humidity was always high and the temperature in the shade varied roughly between 80 and 90 degrees Fahrenheit.

On the higher ground within the Area were Kitchener, Roberts, and Gordon Barracks. Lower down were the Royal Artillery, Wavell, Birdwood and India Lines, the various Messes, Officers' Bungalows and Married Quarters attached to all these, and Changi Village itself. Originally, this total Area was constructed to house one Brigade, but by 20th February 1942 it housed 47,000 British and Australian troops, the Indian troops being segregated in a separate Area, Nee Soon, probably with the intention of forcing them to join the 'Free Indian Army'.

When we arrived at Changi, the whole Area was deserted and had the appearance of a ghost town that had been hastily evacuated by the last residents, and then looted. There was, in reality, plenty of odd material lying about, and all this was gradually recovered and put to good use. In fact, Changi had been heavily bombed, but many of the main buildings were little damaged. However, the sewage system and water supply were largely out of action and the water pumps and electric light system had been destroyed before the evacuation of our own troops.

The first thing to provide was more accommodation, and bamboo-framed huts were erected and covered with canvas and tarpaulins; in fact, anything that would provide cover was used. This was a major task, and even at the end of March seven thousand men were still without proper shelter. Apart from providing more accommodation, it was necessary to build cookhouses, and these we eventually floored with paving slabs, taken up from paths and anti-malarial drains, a measure taken to try to overcome the fly problem.

Overcrowding was at first extreme, but later, in March, April and May large numbers of troops were taken into Singapore, where they were located in various camps, and employed in cleaning up the aftermath of the bombardment and providing labour in the Docks. Another party went to Sime Road Camp, near the MacRitchie Reservoir, to construct a Shinto Shrine, named Shonan Jinjya, which the Japanese envisaged as a symbol of their success in the South. Geoffrey Pharaoh Adams, author of *No Time for Geishas*, was one of those prisoners employed on this project.

The departure of these parties certainly did a lot to relieve the congestion. By the end of March 1942, 5,812 men had been transferred to Singapore, and by June of that year the number of departures had reached 30,000. These men, on the whole, fared better than those in Changi, particularly those working in the Docks where there was ample opportunity for looting, and black markets flourished.

This easing in overcrowding was not to last, as the IJA (Imperial Japanese Army) started to use Changi as a Transit Camp, with bodies of troops from the Dutch East Indies continually arriving, and departing again after a brief stay, either overseas or up country. The hygiene of these parties became a constant source of anxiety to the medical fraternity.

At the outset sanitary arrangements in Changi were non-existent, and flies already prevalent. There were very limited quantities of water available in the lower parts of the camp and these, together with the output of four anti-malarial drains, formed the only sources of supply, and so water had to be drastically rationed to half a gallon per head daily, for all purposes.

In the early days of our captivity we were allowed to go to a nearby beach, in organized parties, to bathe and wash ourselves in the sea, but of course we had no soap. In peace-time no-one would have considered bathing in the open sea without the protection of a pagar, because of sharks, but we had no such luxury. However, I never heard of a shark even being seen.

Morale in general was very low after the capitulation, and because at that time there was little understanding of the importance of strict hygiene, a major epidemic of dysentery broke out within three days, and ultimately there were 16,397 cases during the year, a ratio of 392 per thousand. This figure is extracted from the main Medical Report of POW Camp, Changi 1942/1943. Initially, the spread of disease was through flies, but when men became more hygiene conscious, it was the 'carriers' who spread disease. Later, no-one who had recovered from dysentery was allowed to work in a cookhouse for a period of four months.

The India Lines at Changi were allocated to part of 18th Division, and here we eventually made ourselves reasonably comfortable in the two barrack blocks overlooking the main padang and in the wooden huts the other side. In one barrack block were housed the officers, and in the other the senior NCOs; a barrack block intended for 150 men housed anything from six to eight hundred. The junior NCOs and troops were in the wooden huts, and tents were put up to the north of India Barracks in the 'Java Lines'.

These barrack blocks were two-storey whitewashed concrete buildings, and each one had a veranda running along the whole length of the front. The verandas had open-arched entrances to the inner part which was, in fact, one large room with pillars down the middle supporting the flat roof. Leading off this, at each end, were two bunk rooms, and these were allotted to Lieut-Colonels, although Wilkie merely occupied a bed on the veranda. On each floor there was an ablution block at the back, and all available space, including that on the verandas, was taken up by camp or makeshift beds.

We were near the sea, but could only catch a glimpse of it from some of the higher points in the Changi Area, although we could hear and feel quite clearly the throb of the propellers of the approaching warships, making their way to the Naval Base. We were almost completely surrounded by palm trees, but there were large open spaces which had been parade grounds, recreation grounds and gun parks when it had been a peace-time station. In parts of the camp there were magnificent trees, including durian, breadfruit and the glorious flame-of-the forest, and of course, hibiscus bushes.

The addicted smokers amongst us gathered the leaves of the hibiscus, drying and pressing them into blocks, to make a poor imitation of tobacco. I was glad I had never been a smoker, so the lack of cigarettes did not worry me in the slightest.

There was also a strange parasitic orchid, *Dendrobium Crumenatum* or the Pigeon Orchid, which grew on various host trees in Singapore and throughout South East Asia. The plant was non-seasonal and produced flower buds which developed to a certain stage at which they rested until a sudden drop in temperature, usually the result of a thunderstorm, provided the necessary stimulus to the buds to mature and flower. This process took nine days and the result was that every plant within the area flowered together, which was a wonderful sight.

We became very attached to the geckoes, or chichaks. These little lizards adopted their own territory on the walls and ceilings of our blocks, and they could run about on a ceiling with great agility. They lived on small insects, particularly mosquitoes, which was why we valued them so much. Several 'Tonk-Tonk' birds, or night-jars, lived around the camp, and it became almost an obsession to count the number of 'tonks' they would do at any one time.

A sight that never ceased to fascinate me at Changi was the flood of bats that literally poured out of the palm trees at dusk. One could stand and look at a single tree to see them streaming out in their hundreds; this is probably an exaggeration, but was how it appeared to me. In the tropics there is very little twilight. One minute it is light, and within a few minutes darkness has fallen, and it was in those few minutes between daylight and darkness that all the bats took to the air.

The tropical rains came, with complete regularity, at four o'clock every afternoon, but lasted only a short time. In the early days we would all run out, stark naked, to stand around the edges of the buildings while the water from the roofs poured down on us. As the roofs were flat, and of course, hot in the sun, the rain coming off them made a wonderfully warm shower. We could hear these 'Sumatras' approaching from miles away, and the palm trees bent over in the winds that followed. The anti-malarial drains were flowing to capacity within a few minutes, but as soon as the rains stopped, the ground dried up almost immediately.

After a time, we managed to get the various ablution blocks working and equipped with a water supply, and everything became more civilized than when we had first taken over the Area. We largely overcame the problem of bed-bugs by standing the legs of our beds in small tins or coconut shells, partly filled with palm oil, which prevented any migration of bugs from the floor, once we had cleared our own beds of these pests.

Of course, our only source of power and heat was timber from the palm trees, and there were parties of men permanently cutting, and carting this in trailers, made from the chassis of abandoned vehicles. These were hauled along by teams of men with ropes, and became known as 'Changi trucks'.

The R.E. stores at Changi, though damaged during hostilities, produced spades, changkols, picks and other tools, but more important than most other things were the 13 earth augers, which were distributed throughout the Area for making deep boreholes for the latrines, 16 to 18 inches wide and about 18 feet deep. Without these augers, I just cannot think how we would have tackled our latrine problem.

None of us had any idea how long we should be there. Some prisoners stayed in the Changi Area for three and a half years, until the war ended in the autumn of 1945, whereas others were moved to different camps to work for the Japanese, as I have already mentioned. We were an enormous fund of cheap labour for them, always available, to be used for whatever project they had in mind, and they certainly made the most of exploiting us to the full.

I remained in Changi for 14 months, before being taken to work on the Thailand/Burma railway, and during those 14 months I was much involved with the engineering work and maintenance of Roberts Hospital. I was grateful to have the chance of doing something worthwhile with my time, and of being able to help, indirectly, those men who were in such desperate need of hospital treatment. There is much that I would like to say about Roberts Hospital, and feel that it warrants a chapter of its own. I have, therefore, written a separate section on the hospital, which is in the Appendices; all figures and dates quoted are authoritative, as they are taken from the official Changi Medical Reports of that period.

At first, all troops had full freedom within the camp Area but, later, formations were wired off separately within the confines of their respective barracks, and all inter-communication controlled by the IJA through a system of passes and flags, the sentries being drawn from the Sikhs, who had been coerced into the 'Free Indian Army' (Indian National Army).

In the early days, the Japanese left us very much to ourselves, and apart from the Sikh sentries, whom we passed when going out in groups to cut wood for the cookhouses, and when the *tenko* (roll-call) was taken each evening, we saw very little of them. As the hospital was in a separate Area, I had to wear a pass on an armband, or carry a flag, to go from India Lines to the hospital.

The final indignity came when our senior officers were made to salute the sentries, and even at times, crawl past them on their hands and knees and, although it went against the grain, we had to be very punctilious about saluting.

Until the IJA ration became available on 24th February, food was limited to such as the troops had been able to bring with them. The rations were mainly rice, and very occasionally, blatchang. This was an evil smelling dried fish, which certainly added flavour to the rice! Palm oil seemed to be available at times, and then the cooks surpassed themselves by producing 'doovers', which were balls of rice deep-fried in palm oil. Of course, if a stray dog should be misguided enough to wander into the camp, it never went out again, and was probably made into rissoles.

In April 1942, private purchases of sundry articles, specified by the Japanese, became possible through an Indian contractor appointed to the camp, Gian Singh, and local purchases for the hospital were permitted. At this time the money available for these transactions came from individuals' own private funds, and many illicit deals took place at night, through the perimeter wire, with local Chinese who took incredible risks in so doing.

In June 1942, the IJA started paying an amenity grant of 25 cents daily to officers, 15 cents to NCOs, and 10 cents to Privates, but purchases were limited and very expensive. In September of that year officers first received pay at the rate of 30 dollars a month for Captains and above, 25 dollars for First Lieutenants, and 10.83 dollars for Second Lieutenants. Out of this, deductions of from five to ten dollars made possible the establishment of Hospital and Company Messing Funds, which provided small quantities of rice polishings, whitebait, peanuts and red palm oil, but here again regularity of supply proved a stumbling block.

In October the main bulk of the Red Cross supplies from South Africa was received at the hospital, and for the first time Vitamin B_2 deficiency began to decline, but these supplies were consumed by the end of the year.

In December 1942, most camps in Singapore closed down, and the 10,000 remaining Australian and British prisoners again returned to Changi, others having gone north to Thailand.

Two great advantages were the climate and the quality of the soil, which enabled us to start growing various vegetables, and spinach in particular, normally producing three crops a year; these vegetables added the main variety to our diet. However, the doctors amongst us were becoming very worried about the lack of vitamins in our diet, and the Japanese eventually started to produce sacks of rice polishings. I think no-one would have attempted to take these, had we not all been so afraid of becoming impotent! The only way to get them down was to put them in a mug, add water, and as they were completely insoluble, swill them down; these rice polishings were nauseating and alive with weevils.

Men had been suffering from dysentery and malaria right from the start, and it was very noticeable how most of the British, with their determination to survive, were carried into hospital and eventually returned to our Lines, not cured but perhaps better. They held on to their possessions, whereas others, particularly those from the Dutch East Indies among the cases I knew, gave away their belongings on entering hospital, as they had not the stoic determination to live. Sure enough, many of them died.

I am afraid that a sound which we heard only too often was the playing of the Last Post, although the deaths at this time were few in number compared with later, on the railway. There, there was no Last Post. On these occasions, if we were attending the funeral of a friend, or one of our own Company, we got out our best shirts and shorts to try and make ourselves as smart as possible.

Before arriving in Singapore, it had been impressed on all of us that we should never venture out into the sun without our solar topees, as we would most certainly get sunstroke. However, during all our time on the Equator, with no form of headgear or shirt, I heard of no-one suffering from sunstroke; thus, the solar topee became obsolete.

We settled down into a routine, and the weeks and months dragged on. The news we received through the 'canaries' at that time was always bad, with nothing to give us any encouragement that the war might end. 'Canaries' was the name used for illicit radios, made from any parts that could be scrounged, and hidden in most ingenious places such as hollowed out brushes or holes in the ground. The men who made and ran these put their lives at tremendous risk.

When not on working parties, either gardening or timber hauling, there was much spare time, and various courses in book-keeping, languages, farming and suchlike were initiated. From a nucleus of animals supplied by the Japanese, a piggery was started, and Lord De Ramsey, of 135 Field Regiment, R.A., was head pigman! Incidentally, he had been in my form at Oundle. With the vast number of prisoners, we had specialists in almost every subject, and thus 'Changi University' was formed—the main asset being initiative, as there were very few books and little equipment.

It was not long before soap was being produced, the main constituents being wood ash and palm oil, and eventually, even paper was manufactured in small quantities. Thousands of clogs, known as 'klompers', were made. They had wooden soles, and the bands over the insteps were cut from old rubber tyres. Without these, most of us would have been barefoot within a year. There was no end to the ingenuity of the men. They would have a go at anything, even producing a red substance for the gums of false teeth, made out of a mixture of laterite and latex!

Of course, one must never forget the value of the entertainments put on by the concert parties. A permanent outdoor wooden stage was erected in Changi Village, which was part of India Lines, and for us was just a short walk down the road. The performances that were put on did so much to lift morale, and it could not have been easy being a comedian on stage, in such circumstances, but always popular were our glamorous budding Danny La Rues!

One thing entirely lacking in our captivity was music. Someone in our building had an old portable gramophone, but sadly, only one record! This was 'Night and Day', sung by Maxine Sullivan, and just accentuated our separation from home and families. However, everyone seemed to lap it up, and surely it must have become the most played record in the world!

Facilities for games were not particularly good, but we managed to play cricket and hockey. We scrounged plenty of hockey sticks, but at first could find no balls. We tried tapping rubber trees and making solid balls from the latex, but these were far too heavy and would have broken all the sticks. Eventually, some hockey balls were acquired, from where I know not, so we managed to play hockey fairly often. Some of the British Indian Army people were too good for the rest of us and a great pleasure to watch, and as hockey was always played on the padang in front of our quarters, we were lucky enough to be able to enjoy the matches from our veranda.

Adjacent to our barrack block was an old mosque, which we tidied up for the use of the Division, and our Sappers carved altar rails from teak, which they had acquired. The Padres in the camp then held Communion services every Sunday. Perhaps it has not been sufficiently recognized how helpful these dedicated people were during our POW life. Padre J. N. Duckworth had done a great deal before the capitulation, and had elected to stay behind with some of the wounded of his regiment at Batu Pahat. He was a great person, and having coxed the crew in the 1936 Olympic Games, kept us amused with stories of the Games when, in those days, there was a somewhat different attitude to sport. He welcomed men of all denominations and religions, and thus drew tremendous congregations, and I am glad to say that he survived the war, and later became a Canon. He died only recently.

One of the Japanese officers in charge of us at that time was a Christian, and he made arrangements for the Bishop of Singapore to come from his place of imprisonment, Changi Gaol, to India Lines to perform a Confirmation ceremony. This was the Rt. Rev. Dr. John Leonard Wilson, who survived his imprisonment, and later became the Bishop of Birmingham. He was indeed a brave man, who stood up to severe torture by the Kempei-Tai at their headquarters in Singapore, and after the war his message to us was that we should 'forgive but not forget'.

Books were few and far between, and were of course very precious, but we were able to start a small library from those that had been left behind. I became fascinated with the design of yachts, and learnt quite a lot from a Dutch naval architect, who also taught me the theory of celestial navigation. He had been lucky enough to find a copy of Reid's *Nautical Almanack*, or some equivalent book, and also a set of log tables left behind by the previous occupants of the Area, and I made a very simple type of sextant out of a piece of plywood and a small plumb bob.

I badly wanted to try and produce a spirit by distillation, but unfortunately this was something expressly forbidden by the IJA. However, I found a supply of overripe pineapples, which I cut up and put in a five-gallon drum, with water. To this I added some bruised bean-shoots, which some expert informed me would act as a diastase, and then allowed it all to ferment. From the copper brake tubes of blown-up lorries I produced a coil condenser, and attached it to the lid of the five-gallon drum, under which I then built a fire, and cooled the condenser by trickling water over it, being careful to catch the waste in order to use it again. It was terribly exciting when a clear liquid started to drip from the end of the condenser pipe. We were still able to find a few limes growing in the Area, and on Sunday mornings we drank our neat alcohol and lime cocktails! After a time I gave this up, as it became too dangerous when too many people knew about it.

One would think that there would have been a great deal of homosexuality among many thousands of men crowded together in captivity. However, as far as I knew, this was not the case, owing, I believe, to our poor state of health and low vitality, and in all the time I was at Changi, I never once came across it. Lethargy had eroded all sexual feeling, but we all felt a strong bond of friendship.

As time passes, it is the highs and the lows that one remembers and, strangely enough, there were things of great beauty as well as appalling horror. As in life, the mediocre does not live long. In the evenings we often climbed to the top of the hill, where lay the remains of the huge 15-inch guns that were supposed to have made Singapore an impregnable fortress, but whose limited arc of fire rendered them useless. From here we stood and watched the most beautiful sunsets that I have seen anywhere in the world, and we looked expectantly for that green flash that so many say occurs at the disappearance of the sun, but I am not convinced that I have ever seen it. Some said that these sunsets were so magnificent because of the dust particles remaining in the atmosphere from the eruption of the volcano, Krakatoa, which happened so long ago. This seemed a most unlikely story, the air being so clear that we could see Venus at midday.

At night, when all the lights were out and most men were asleep, three or four of us often climbed through an opening on to the roof, where we sat with our legs hanging over the edge, talking well into the night, while watching the stars and the bright moon. The moon, I felt, was my one contact with

home, as it was the same moon that Lindsay would later see
in Wales. Being on the Equator, we could also see the Southern
Cross, which meant so much to the Australians. Occasionally,
a Japanese patrol walked past, and so we drew back from the
edge of the roof and remained silent until they had gone. I
think I shall always remember these peaceful hours on the
roof at night, sometimes by myself and sometimes with
others. It was a time when one thought about home, 'above'
the realities of the prison camp.

While we were in Changi a few letters arrived from home.
It was expressly forbidden by the Japanese to receive photographs, but Lindsay did enclose one or two snapshots of
Roger and herself in the two letters which reached me that
year, and these I treasured greatly and still have today.

After about 12 months, we were allowed to send one postcard home, with a limited number of words on it. There was
nothing very much one could say in so few words, especially
bearing in mind that they would be censored. We didn't want
to worry our families with news of our living conditions, and
I remember that Wilkie, in his postcard to his wife, merely
said: 'Tell the Marines the food is wonderful. Love, Mike.'
The card I wrote was the one and only postcard that Lindsay
ever received from me, as after my attempted escape I was
not allowed to send any further cards, being in the hands of
the Kempei-Tai (Japanese Military Police). This, of course,
gave her more grounds for worry, as she was in touch with
wives of other prisoners, who had received three more cards
during the three and a half years of captivity.

After the fall of Singapore on 15th February 1942, our
families were notified that we were missing, believed prisoners of war, and I learnt after the war that this information
had caused Lindsay to have a miscarriage. It was not until
Christmas Eve of that year that she finally received official
notification that I had, in fact, been taken prisoner when
Singapore fell. In the meantime, she advertised in both the
National and Australian press, asking if any of those who had
left Singapore before the capitulation had any knowledge of
me, and as a result of this, received a cable from Capt.
Harradine, telling her that I had been alive a few days prior
to the cessation of hostilities. He was our Senior Subaltern

who had left with the official escape party prior to the fall of Singapore. I felt that my worries were less than Lindsay's, because I knew that she and Roger were living in as safe a place as possible in North Wales, but she, on the other hand, knew nothing of my whereabouts and conditions.

On one occasion, a very high-ranking Japanese General decided to make an inspection of all Allied prisoners, and every man able to walk was made to line the main road approaching Changi. Here we stood for hours in the scorching sun, awaiting his arrival. I don't think it can have been a very edifying inspection for him, as all he saw were thousands of ill-dressed men, facing outwards from the road; we were not allowed to look either at him or his entourage.

It may seem odd, but I remember that we had a lot of laughter at this stage of our captivity. I think we were lucky in that several of us, and particularly Wilkie, had what proved to be a life-saving sense of humour; we were lulled into a false sense of security. On looking back, I think the content of our humour cannot have been very high, but we had almost reached the state of mind when anything which was not mundane made us laugh. Perhaps it was nervous laughter.

There was, however, the permanent rumour that the Japanese could no longer feed us, that we had become an embarrassment to them, and that we were to be sent to Lourenço Marques in Mozambique, which was a neutral country, but this, of course, never came about.

(ii) The Selarang Incident

In August 1942 the IJA issued an order stating that all senior officers above the rank of Lieutenant-Colonel, and any other officers with a University Engineering Degree, would be transferred to Formosa (Taiwan). Both Wilkie and I had degrees, but he thought it better for us to remain quiet about this, so that we could stay with our own troops, and I could continue my work for the hospital. Until this time General Percival had administered the camp, but now Major-General Fukuei arrived and took over.

General Fukuei immediately decided that all POWs should sign a 'parole', agreeing not to attempt an escape. Four escapees—two Australians and two British—had left Bukit

Timah Camp, but had been recaptured after rowing miles in a small boat, and this incident may have been the reason for forcing us to sign the parole.

All men knew that such a paper was illegal, and refused to sign it, but General Fukuei was adamant, and ordered that all troops should be concentrated in Selarang Barracks within four hours of the issue of a movement order.

The warning order was received at 0200 hours on 2nd September 1942 and the movement order at 1400 hours. All troops had, therefore, to be in the allotted Area by 1800 hours with whatever kit they could carry or move by hand trucks. Initially, the order had included 2,435 patients in Roberts Hospital, but on a strong appeal this was rescinded. Even so, there were hundreds of unfit who could not be admitted to hospital, and so had to march the two miles to Selarang.

Before the war Selarang had housed a battalion of the Gordons, and the overall dimensions of the Area were 800 feet by 400 feet, and the only permanent structures available in the Area were seven barrack blocks, each with three floors, 150 feet by 60 feet, including verandas and staircases; 850 men occupied each floor, which meant 10 square feet per person, and many men were camping on the roofs of the buildings and out on the square, without any shelter from sun and rain, and only a few feet from the latrines. The Area was bounded by the inner margin of a road circumscribing the Area, with machine guns at each corner, covering all four sides of the rectangle.

The concentration area excluded all previous latrine accommodation; thus the only place available for latrines was the heavily macadamized square. An immediate start was made to break through the tough surface and the hardcore below, but with so many dysentery sufferers, a certain amount of soiling was unavoidable in the earlier stages.

Three water points were available, one being a concrete well, and the other two being taps from a rising main. The numbers of men which these three points had to supply was 15,400, 13,350 being British and the remaining 2,050 Australian. However, some reports put the total as 17,000.

Therefore, water was very strictly rationed, and washing facilities were non-existent.

Amidst all this deprivation a concert party put on a show that first evening, their stage being the platform of a Changi truck, our normal form of transport for fuel for the cook-houses. I think this was something that our guards just could not understand. The pluck of these men in such appalling conditions was totally incomprehensible to them.

General Fukuei, intent on breaking the deadlock, cut our bare rations to one third. He then took several senior officers to a nearby beach, where they were forced to witness the brutal execution of the four recaptured escapees, by an inefficient firing squad of Sikhs, who were made to fire and fire again when the men pleaded to their executioners to put them out of their misery. Major-General Fukuei was himself executed, more humanely, on 27th April 1946 at exactly the same spot.

The Medical Authorities became increasingly fearful for the health of the troops. Eleven thousand cases of dysentery had occurred in Changi, and the presence of innumerable carriers at Selarang was inevitable. The nature of the ground was a laterite clay, which was completely impervious to percolation, and therefore the latrines filled up almost immediately, and flooded after rain. Other diseases were also rife, including septic skin diseases, owing to close contact and lack of washing facilities.

In view of all this, and the fact that diphtheria was now a serious problem, and all dead had to be buried within our narrow confines, Lt.-Col. E. B. Holmes of the Manchester Regiment, who was the most senior officer remaining, took the responsibility for ordering us all to sign the 'parole', on 5th September 1942. Having done so, we were then allowed to return to Changi.

We attached no importance to this 'parole', as we had signed under duress, and I suspect the signatures on those forms bore little resemblance to our normal ones. This whole episode has passed down into history as 'The Selarang Incident', and it has been said that this was the closest concentration of human beings since the Black Hole of Calcutta.

Map 3.   Map of the Thailand/Burma Railway

NOTATION
P.O.W. Railway
State Railways
Burma/Thai
    Border
Escape Route

KILOMETRE CHART OF THE THAILAND TO BURMA RAILWAY

NOTE: POW often gave English style names to places, the Japanese adapted Thai names to their own pronunciation. Several names are given to help all readers.

LOCATIONS ON RAILWAY 1942 - 1945 — Distances from NONG PLADUK

000 km	NONG PLADUK, Nonpuradokku
002	Konma (transit camp)
005	Ban Pong, Banponmai
013	Rukke
026	Taruanoi, To Reoa Noi, Talua
039	Tha Muang, Tamuang, Tamoan, Ta Mueng
041	Tung Tung
047	Kao Din
048	Pak Prage
049	Tung Na Talea
051	KANCHANABURI, Kanburi
055	THA MAKHAM, Tamarkan (River Kwae Restaurant) River Kwae Yai/Mae Khlaung
057	Chungkai, Kao Poon, Kaopon
069	Wang Lan, Wanran, Wun Lung
078	Tapon, Won Yen, Wang Yen
088	Bankao, Bangkao
098	Takiren, Tarkilen, Ta Ki Len
108	Arrowhill, Arruhiru (Wang Sing)
110	Lum Sum (for waterfall)
114	Wang Po, Wanpo, Wampo (double viaduct)
121	Chong Cab
125	Wanyai, Wang Yai
130	THA SOE, Tarso, Ta Soe
130**	NAM TOK (Railway ends 1978)
139	Tonchan (spring camp)
147	Tampi, Tampines
155	Hin Tok, Hintoku
166	Kanu, Kanyu (several camps)
168	Sai Yoku, Kinsaiyok sub-camps
172	Kinsaiyok Main (waterfalls)
181	Rin Tin, Rinten, Lin Thin
190	Kuei, Kui Ye, Kui Yong
198	Hin Dat, Hindato (hot springs)
208	Brankassi, Purankasi, Prang Kasi
218	Takunun, Dha Khanun, Takanun
229	Namajon, Namajo, Namuchonyai
237	Tomajo, Tamajo, Tamazyo
244	Tamuron Part, Tamuronpato
250	Krian Kri, Kuriankurai, Kreung Krai
258	Kurikonta
262	Konkuita, Konkoita, Concreeta
262.87	MEETING POINT 17 OCTOBER 1943
273	Teimonta, Timontar

282	Nikhe, Nikki, Nike
294	Sonkurai, Songkla, Keungkluay
HERE IS THREE PAGODAS PASS	Thailand/Burma border
301 km	Changaraya
311	Anganan, Aungganaung
315	"100 Kilo" Camp, Anganan 2
320	Kyando, Kyondaw
332	Aparon, Apalon
- -	Steel Bridge
337	Aparain
343	Mezari, Mezali, Mesali
349	Kami-Mezari, "Upper Mezali"
354	Ronsi, Ronshi
358	Tanzun, Taungzun
362	Tunbaya, Tambaya ("Hospital")
369	Anakuin, Anaqueen, Anankwin
375	Bekitan, Beke Taung
385	Repo, Retpu
391	Konnokoi
396	Rabao, Alepauk
401	Tettoku
406	Wegare, Wegale SIN-TANBYUZAYA "New Thanbyuzayat"
414.92 km	THANBYUZAYAT Burma Base Camp

		From Moulmein
421 km	Kuwanra	
429	Karuoto, Kawawthut	43 km
433	Kamae, Kamawet	38 km
439	Toku, Tawku	32 km
447	Mudon	24 km
453	Menganen	19 km
461	Pau, Pa-Nuk	11 km
466	Kokani	6 km
471.30 km	MOULMEIN, Morumein	0 km

BRANCH LINE THANBYUZAYAT TO YE:-

THANBYUZAYAT	000 km (going South)
Banga	9
Karotsuhe, Karokpi	14
Anke	19
Tenyu	26
Atsunein	35
Nikkayin	45
Ramayin	55
Karunpe, Taungban	65
Painwan	71
Paraenki	78
YE	** 86.40 km

Thailand POW Groups : 1, 2, 4, 6, 'F' Force, 'H' Force.
Burma POW Groups : 3, 5.
Medical Groups : 'K' Force, 'L' Force.

Chapter 5

THAILAND

(i) Departures in 1942/3

PARTIES BEGAN leaving Changi in 1942 for unknown destinations. In May 1942 the so-called 'A' Force, of 3,000 Australians under Brigadier A. L. Varley, left by sea, to Burma as it turned out, for aerodrome construction work initially, and thence in October to Thanbyuzayat, the Burma base of the proposed new railway. In June the 'Mainland' party of 3,000, all British, left Singapore station in five train-loads, the first leaving on 18th June. These proved destined for Ban Pong at the head of the Gulf of Siam, thence to work on the new railway. In October large parties, all British, left from Sime Road, Adam Park, Changi Village and Changi, totalling 14,260, all detraining at Ban Pong.

In 1943 parties leaving for Ban Pong from January to mid-April were of mixed nationalities—British, Australian and Dutch—totalling 17,760. As in 1942, all these parties were transferred from Singapore Japanese administration to Thai/Burma Japanese administration.

On 18th April the ill-starred 'F' Force under Lt.-Col. S. W. Harris, R.A., began to leave Changi in 13 train-loads, also destined for Ban Pong but never transferred to Thai/Burma Japanese administration. 'F' Force comprised 3,334 British and 3,666 Australians. On 5th May, also never transferred to Thai/Burma administration, 'H' Force began to leave under Lt.-Col. H. R. Humphries, R.A., comprising 1,411 British, 670 Australians and 588 Dutch. Two further small medical parties of mixed nationalities, 'K' Force and 'L' Force, left on 25th June and 24th August respectively.

Major-General Arimura, G.O.C. Allied Prisoners of War in Malaya, issued orders that 'F' Force was to be composed of

3,600 Australians and 3,400 British. The actual order issued
by his headquarters was:

1. The reason for the move was that the food situation in
   Singapore was difficult, and that it would be far better
   in the new place.
2. This was not a working party.
3. As there were not seven thousand fit combatants in
   Changi, thirty per cent of the party were to be 'unfit'
   men, unfit to march or work. The unfit men would have
   a better chance of recovery with better food, and in a
   pleasant hilly country, with good facilities for recreation.
4. There would be no marching, except for short distances
   from train to nearby camp, and transport would be
   provided for baggage, and men unfit to march.
5. The Band were to be taken.
6. All tools and cooking gear, and an engine and gear for
   electric light were to be taken.
7. Gramophones, blankets, clothing and mosquito nets
   would be issued at the new camps.
8. A good canteen would be available in each camp after
   three weeks. Canteen supplies for the first three weeks
   were to be bought with prisoners' money before leaving
   Singapore.
9. The party would include a Medical Party of about three
   hundred and fifty, with equipment for a central hospital
   of four hundred patients, and a medical supply for three
   months.

As a general rule, the fitter elements of the population of
Changi had been sent on the earlier parties, but with the
promise of better conditions and the fact that there were
fewer men left in Changi, about two thousand unfit men
were included in 'F' Force, and even the remaining 5,000 had
also had some kind of medical history since the capitulation,
many of them being recent convalescents from such diseases
as diphtheria, dysentery and beri-beri. All were reduced in
strength already by malnutrition during the previous year.

In April 1943, when I had been at Changi for 14 months,
we received the order to provide this party of 7,000 men,

including thirty per cent unfit men from the hospital, to go to other prison camps where food and living conditions would be better. The Japs were adept at making empty promises. This meant that all the remaining Sappers had to go to make up the numbers, and so Wilkie and I went with them, leaving on 24th April. Before departing, I took the precaution of getting the Sappers in the hospital workshop to hide my compass under a false bottom in my water bottle, just in case.

Looking back on our time in Changi, we had not suffered too badly, apart from isolated incidents. We lacked a balanced diet and the ration of rice we were given was barely enough to keep us going, but we gradually adapted to the limited meals and I don't remember feeling really desperate for food; variety, yes, that was another thing.

We lacked chairs, but became adept at squatting, and in this position we held long conversations, conversation having become the major part of our lives. Otherwise, we lay on our beds, reading.

Uncertainty was our greatest problem, and it was soul-destroying not to be certain of even the smallest things of life. A criminal is sentenced to a term of imprisonment and knows that he will eventually be free, no matter how long his sentence, and he also knows how his family is faring. We had no such knowledge.

In our uncertainty, thank God we did not know of the certainties to come.

(ii) Journey to Ban Pong

By the time 'F' Force left Changi in April 1943 to work on the railway, the Japanese were extremely anxious to get this vast project completed as quickly as possible; other prisoners had already been working on it for six months, but earlier parties had been involved in the general preparation of sites at Nong Pladuk, for sidings, workshops and a labour camp, since June 1942.

Earlier, in peacetime, the possibility of such a railway, from Nong Pladuk to Thanbyuzayat, had been surveyed for the Thai Government by a German team, but the idea was

discarded as being totally uneconomic, owing to the mountainous jungle terrain through which it would have to be
built. However, the Japs wished to transport troops and
supplies overland through to Burma, in preparation for their
invasion of India, as the sea route had now become too risky.
And they were in a hurry.

They were not concerned that machinery for the construction work could not be brought in because of the nature of
the terrain. The Japanese didn't need machinery; they had a
vast source of slave labour at their disposal, that they could
drive on until they dropped in their tracks, and when the
numbers dwindled through disease and starvation, they
brought in more.

The railway was, therefore, built by manpower, using hand
tools (picks, changkols, shovels and explosives), all material
being local except for the actual steel rails and the steel
sections of the bridge at Tha Makham, and the steel sections
of the six steel bridges in Burma over the Zami, Apalon,
Mezali, Winyan, Khonkhau and Myettaw rivers. Sleepers
were made of locally grown and prepared timber, mainly
teak, and some of the ballast was rock chippings from the
cuttings, the remainder being brought in by truck from river
dredgings.

And so the great 'Speedo' was on, and all the prisoners
they could muster, even the sick, were brought in their
thousands to toil on this seemingly impossible feat of en-
deavour.

C. E. Escritt states: 'Personnel employed on the railway
included approximately 10,000 Japanese military, 61,106
prisoners of war, and 182,948 Asiatic coolies. Of the prisoners of war, 12,399 were recorded as having died before
leaving Thailand and Burma'.

Originally, the railway was to have taken 18 months to
build, but the Japs were in such a hurry that, amazingly,
it was completed in a year. It was the Japanese engineers
who were the true masters of the railway, and the IJA camp
administrators could do little but supply the numbers of men
required by the engineers. This is why so many sick men were
sent out to work.

The 182,948 Asian workers, to whom the Japanese paid the mere sum of a Straits dollar a day, were simple country people, having little idea of hygiene, and so cholera and malaria broke out and became rife very quickly. They were ignorant of the necessity to bury their dead efficiently, and the combination of contaminated ground and flies caused their numbers to decrease very rapidly; in all, it has been estimated that over 90,000 coolies died working on the railway.

The IJA were asked to stop the movement of parties, in order to limit the spread of disease, but this was refused, and so cholera spread along the whole upper length of Thailand, affecting the Allied prisoners equally badly, especially 'F' Force, of whom 570 men died immediately after reaching their destination, and 480 died later of various diseases, having recovered from the actual attack of cholera.

Our group of 7,000 men, known as 'F' Force, proved to be the most ill-fated of all such parties to leave Singapore, 'ill-fated' being the adjective applied over and over again in the official medical reports. We went to the most northerly of all camps on the railway in Thailand, and with 'H' Force, who followed us, our living quarters were merely clearings in the jungle, miles from any habitation. Our camps had previously been occupied by coolies, most of whom had died of disease, malnutrition and malaria.

During the latter part of April 1943, each day for 13 days, 600 men left Singapore by train; and still we had no idea of where we were going. At the station we were crowded into steel rice trucks, which were totally enclosed and unventilated apart from double sliding doors in the centre of one side. Thirty-one men were allocated to each truck, and we were packed like sardines; the only way that we could all sit was with our legs tightly drawn in.

We had no form of sanitation, apart from making use of the sliding door, which had a chain stretched across the opening, and on to which we used to hang precariously as the train went along. Many of our numbers had acute dysentery and were passing up to 20 or more motions a day. Gradually, they became too weak to hang out of the door unaided, and

I think many would have fallen out, had they not been helped by others.

With the sun beating down, the heat became intense and we all suffered from severe thirst. I began to wonder whether I had been foolish by having had my compass built into my water bottle, and thus having lost some of its precious capacity. However, at night the truck cooled down, and sometimes we even felt cold.

I think, although I do not remember quite clearly, that twice a day we stopped at small country stations, where we were fed a little rice and had the opportunity to queue for the primitive squatter-type latrines. Whatever else we did, we tried to refill our water bottles, and occasionally were allowed to buy a mug of lime juice.

Many times we pulled into sidings to allow passenger or troop trains to continue unhindered on their way, and sometimes we stopped out in the country between stations, where we were permitted to disembark and do physical exercises to try and keep our circulation going. Without these halts in the country, sanitary conditions in the trucks would have been even worse.

For three days we travelled through Malaya, via Johore, Kuala Lumpur and Prai (opposite Penang Island), through unending rubber estates. Then, after the old Thai border, north of Penang, we passed through miles and miles of flat paddy fields for the next two days, and up the east coast of the Isthmus of Kra, until we arrived at Ban Pong station, which was five kilometres from Nong Pladuk, on the main Bangkok–Singapore railway. Nong Pladuk was the point from which the Thailand/Burma line started, and the reference point for all measurements. We had been unable to sleep, except fitfully, throughout the whole journey, and for the last 24 hours had been given no food or water.

Ban Pong was about sixty kilometres west of Bangkok, and it was here that we disembarked and unloaded our heavy gear, including most of our medical supplies, all of which was to remain, completely unguarded, in a huge dump at the station. Nearly all of these supplies were lost to the Force, as the monsoon broke and the IJA were unable to move any of it

The Author, James
..dley, taken in 1940 before
..g overseas.

Lindsay and Roger, 1940.

3.   The Surrender, 15 February 1942; the arrival at Ford Factory, Bukit Timah, 4.30
On the extreme left, the rifle and bayonet of an I.J.A. guard; (*left to right*) Capt. C. H.
Wild (Ox. & Bucks L. I.), carrying the white flag; Brig. K. S. Torrance, B.G.S. Malaya
Command; Lt. Col. Ichiji Sugita, Intelligence Officer, 25 Army, I.J.A. (later C.O.S.,
J.G.S.D.F., 1961); Lt. Hishikari, I.J.A., Interpreter; Brig. T. K. Newbigging, D.A.G.
Malaya Command; Lt. Gen. A. E. Percival, G.O.C. Malaya Command, 1941/42 (G. P.
Adams Collection).

Roberts Barracks before hostilities (G. P. Adams Collection).

Photograph of Lindsay and Roger, received at Changi. Lindsay sent me this photo as a
stcard. It was posted from Colwyn Bay on 16th August 1942, after she had received
: cable from Capt. Harradine, telling her that I had been alive in February, just before
: capitulation. The picture shows Lindsay, her mother and Roger having a picnic by a
:am. Roger had fallen in and was wearing Lindsay's jersey instead of his wet trousers!
is photograph remained with me the whole time, except when it was confiscated by my
ards.

6. Two bridges at Tha Makham, over the River Mae Khlaung (Kwae Yai), 1945/46 (G. P. Adams Collection).

7. Hintok Bridge, taken in 1945 by a Dutch P.o.W., and typical of many bridges b to take the railway (G. P. Adams Collection).

he Three Pagodas (G. P. Adams
ction).

9.   C5631 locomotive in opening ceremony
of Thailand/Burma railway at Konkuita,
25 October 1943 (Oigawa Railway,
G. P. Adams Collection).

C5631 locomotive at Yasukuni Shrine, Tokyo, from 1979 (G. P. Adams Collection).

11. Changi Gaol, 1980 (Kevin Patience).

12. Roger, aged five years, with a friend, Penny Knowles. Taken in September 1943, this photograph was awaiting me at Changi, where I was taken after my solitary confinement in Outram Road Gaol.

COLONEL
C.H.D. WILD. MBE.
THE OXFORDSHIRE AND
BUCKINGHAMSHIRE LIGHT INF.
25TH SEPTEMBER 1946 AGE 38

13.   The grave of Col. C. H. D. Wild, M.B.E., killed in an air
accident at Hong Kong on 25 September 1946, aged 38 (G. P.
Adams Collection).

14. Jim, Lindy, Timothy and Sarah, October 1981.

by lorry, even if they had ever intended to do so, and how sorely they were to be needed later.

We were marched to Ban Pong Camp, about a kilometre away, but even this short distance was a difficult journey for the really unfit, who had come straight out of hospital in Changi. We had already begun to feel that we were not heading for the good rest camps, which the Japs had promised when telling us to take such a large percentage of unfit with us. As soon as we entered the camp, which turned out to be the base camp for all parties going to work on the railway, our hearts sank.

The camp lay on both sides of a road, and all accommodation consisted of crude bamboo-framed huts, roofed with attap (plaited palm leaves). Down the centre of each was a gangway, flanked on both sides by raised bamboo platforms about six to seven feet wide, and on these we had to live and sleep, almost touching each other. The huts were crawling with bed bugs, and the whole camp was inches deep in black mud. Flies were everywhere, and the approach to the latrines was a morass, with the trenches of the latrines overflowing and alive with dirty grey-white maggots.

There was a 'hospital' hut, but this was sited in the lowest part of the camp and consequently flooded, forming a breeding ground for mosquitoes.

We were given one night's rest before setting out on a 15-stage march of 300 kilometres, although I doubt if many of us got much sleep in such appalling conditions. I know I didn't. We had brought with us our few personal possessions, but, of course, had to abandon most of these, as those amongst us who were still reasonably fit would obviously have to help others who were unable to march unaided. Before leaving, we underwent a very thorough search, but nothing of any consequence was found, and I still had my water bottle with its hidden compass, and my concealed collar stud compass.

I think that Col. (then Capt.) Cyril H. D. Wild, in his report, *Narrative of 'F' Force in Thailand, April–December 1943*, describes the conditions of this march so well that I would like to quote his words:

'The march of three hundred kilometres which followed would have been arduous for fit troops in normal times. For this Force, burdened with its sick and short of food, it proved a trial of unparalleled severity. The road had a loose metal surface for the first two stages, but then degenerated into an old elephant track before widening into a hazardous dry weather trail, through dense and mountainous jungle.

'The march was carried out in stages of twenty to thirty kilometres, and lasted two and a half weeks. The parties always marched at night; the monsoon broke in earnest soon after the march began, and conditions rapidly worsened. Everyone was loaded to capacity and such medical equipment of the Force as could be carried was distributed to individuals.

'Men toiled through the pitch blackness and torrential rain, sometimes knee-deep in water, sometimes staggering off bridges in the dark; sprains and bruises were common, fractures of arms and legs occurred, and stragglers were set upon and looted by marauding Thais. Of the large and growing number of sick, many fell by the wayside, and they and their kit had to be carried by their comrades.

'At the staging-camps, which were merely roadside clearings in the jungle, there was no overhead cover; it was sometimes a long carry for water, and it was impossible for men to rest properly. Food generally consisted of rice and onion stew, with hot water to drink, and often of rice only. This was insufficient to maintain health and entirely inadequate to support the physical strain of a march of this description. These staging-camps were in charge of truculent Japanese NCOs, who demanded large fatigue parties when the men should have been resting, and forcibly drove the sick onto the road with blows, to continue the march night after night, in spite of the protests of their officers.'

(iii) The 300-Kilometre March

When we set off on our march, we had no idea how long it would be, and soon we saw a Buddhist temple on the flat muddy plains through which we walked towards Kanchanaburi (Kanburi to all POWs). We reached Kanburi, 51 kms. from Nong Pladuk on the Thailand/Burma railway, in two days, and we could see the chimneys of the paper factory there. After this, we started walking by night and resting by day, as the heat was so intense during the hours of sunlight. Water was very short in many camps, and at Kanburi we even had to buy drinking water. Lt.-Col. S. W. Harris, R.A., Senior British Officer of 'F' Force, protested strongly about this, but to no avail.

At Tha Makham we crossed over the wide and fast-flowing River Mae Khlaung by a wooden bridge, which was completed as a temporary measure before the main steel one was built alongside it. (Crossing bridges was a precarious business, as we could see the waters beneath us while stepping gingerly along the sleepers.) The steel one was, however, under construction when we passed through, and this bridge became famous after the making of the fictional film, *The Bridge over the River Kwai*, in 1957, and a tourist attraction for Thailand.

I can't help feeling sad that the railway has since become such a tourist attraction, when the cost in human lives in completing this mammoth task was in the region of 116,000. Do the visitors realize this, I wonder, as they take their joy rides up the river? Today, the line remains only as far as Nam Tok (known as Tarsao by POWs), 130 kms., the rest having been dismantled and swallowed up by jungle, as have been thousands of unmarked and unknown graves of men who toiled so hard to construct it.

It is ironic that many POWs lost their lives as a result of Allied bombing. British and American squadrons were detailed to bomb the line, so that it could not be used by the Japanese for their intended purpose, and as the camps were so close to the line, the prisoners were unable to avoid these attacks.

C. E. Escritt, in his notes of May 1981, says:

'The Mae Khlaung bridge was attacked ten times between 29th November 1944, and 28th July 1945, by both USAAF and RAF, the most successful attack being that of 13th February 1945, when three of the eleven steel spans fell and most of the re-built wooden bridge was destroyed.'

This necessitated the keeping of a permanent POW labour force for effecting repairs to these bridges.

Our journey took us along the left, or east, bank of the Kwae Noi (the Little Kwae), and at first the track was not too bad. We passed through open country with fields cultivated for peanuts, but soon we ran into more hilly country, with clumps of elephant grass and bamboo thickets.

We came to Chungkai, 57 kms., and here an enormous cutting and embankment was being worked, and in the process was taking a huge toll of lives. It should really have been a tunnel, but the equipment and men needed were not available, so men were working non-stop, in long shifts, to dig away this incredible amount of rock. During the nights the Japs had officer POWs operating hand-turned generators for artificial lighting, at bayonet point.

Before reaching Wampo, 114 kms., we crossed two timber viaducts, clinging to the vertical face of the rock, with a drop of 20 to 30 feet into the river below. These were fantastic feats of engineering, and although 400 feet long, they had been completed in just 17 days, by 2,000 POWs. Many men had fallen to their deaths from the rock face, but the Japanese had shown scant concern for the loss of these human lives. The Wampo viaducts still stand today, in 1981, taking two trains a day.

After Wampo, the country became wilder, with jungle spreading right down to the river. We reached Tarsao, 130 kms., a large base headquarters camp, on the sixth day, and were allowed one day's rest. It was at Tarsao where Capt. Wild and Major Bruce Hunt, an Australian doctor from Perth, were badly beaten up when they pleaded for 36 men to be left at the camp, as they were too ill to carry on. The doctor's hand was broken. The men were made to continue with their party, and most of them died shortly afterwards.

We did not go into any of the camps we passed, supposedly because the Japs were worried that we were spreading disease, but were provided by the inmates of those camps with whatever they could spare in the way of food and water. We had now walked 130 kilometres, and had been able to leave a few sick men at various camps on the way, but they had to be almost dying before the Japanese would allow them to be left. All the time they were driving on any stragglers who fell behind, simply because they had not the strength to keep up with the main body. Others with dysentery had of necessity to keep stopping, but they too were kicked on. We all tried to help each other, either by carrying other men's packs or by trying to support them physically.

Here again, my admiration for our doctors was quite unbounded. First they would be called to a casualty falling back at the rear of the column, and next they would be wanted up front. When we arrived at our staging camps, completely without shelter, we would throw ourselves on the ground and perhaps take off our boots, if we dared, because of the fear of not being able to put them on again. The doctors, however, held sick parades, attending to men's blistered and burnt feet, and doing what they could for the sick and dying. They took little time to rest themselves, but I believe they received scant recognition for all they did, except in the gratitude which showed on the faces of all those whom they helped.

And thus we went on, normally marching from 7.00 p.m. to 7.00 a.m., getting more weary all the way, and losing more sick at any camp that would accept them. Each night we trudged for approximately 25 kilometres, and during the day slept in the open, regardless of weather. Past Hintok, 155 kms., an Australian mountain camp, and on to Kinsaiyok, 172 kms., along narrow tracks blasted out of the rock face to take the line. The terrain was more mountainous and many were the cuttings blasted out of the rock. We had now completed 170 kilometres, although we did not know it at the time, and so we did not realize that some of us still had another 130 kilometres to go before reaching our final destination.

'F' Force trudged past Kinsaiyok, 172 kms., for days, but were not allowed to enter the camp because cholera was already an epidemic there. From this and other diseases 300 out of 900 died in a period of six months. G. P. Adams says:

'At this time, however sorry we may have been for ourselves, our hearts could bleed for the unfortunates of 'F' Force who passed by our camp for days on end. Sometimes separated from each other by battalions of Japanese infantrymen, all were tired and worn, the Japs dragging themselves towards their promised victory in Burma.

'These young Jap reinforcements would also pull along their 70 mm battalion artillery pieces, and ammunition, occasionally aided by pitifully thin horses and mules. We did not know it then, but not one in ten of them would survive the next two years of war in Burma, and we would not have cared had we known!

"F' Force were sent from Changi to aid the 'speedo', and replace those who had died on the earlier Siam work groups. Told at Changi they were going to a good rest camp, they had amongst their numbers sick men and even some senior officers had been enticed from the tedium of Changi. Among them was our own Driver 'Tessa' Turner, a mere wasted shell of his former self; I found him collapsed outside our own camp area—they were not allowed inside due to our cholera outbreak. We found water for him, and some food, but he was not really interested.

'Tessa died a few kilometres up the track. A Thai had come to him and offered to carry his pack. Our man, unwary of the perils of the jungle, in desperation agreed, only to see the Thai run off into the bamboo forest leaving him bereft of warmth and comfort. His friend, too weak to aid, could only report the event to an officer. Perhaps 'Tessa' was better off to go when he did for 'F' Force faced greater trials than any on the Railway of Death.'

To us, Kinsaiyok looked beautiful, with the barges on the river, which we could see by the light of a huge moon; all appeared peaceful under the thousands of bright stars.

By contrast, the next camp, Rin Tin, 181 kms., was foul with a stink of dirt and decay, and here no bird sang. The Japanese had closed the camp, owing to the unacceptable death rate from dysentery; 231, mainly Dutch, had died out of a complement of 900.

I think it must have been Hindato, 198 kms., where we were allowed to rest for about an hour, and here we stripped off and sat revelling in the hot springs near the river. This was almost the first wash we had enjoyed since leaving Changi, and we were now in the hottest month of the year, with temperatures reaching well over 100 degrees Fahrenheit in the shade.

On reading C. E. Escritt's notes of May 1981, I see that: 'During the Pacific War the only known use made of the hot springs sanatorium near Hin Dat was by comfort girls, sent up for Japanese soldiers and Korean *heiho*.' (In 1944 G. P. Adams reported that a party of one officer and 19 other ranks went daily, as a fatigue party, to the brothel.)

On we went, past many more working camps, through what was now much more difficult and mountainous country, until we came to Konkuita, at the 262 kms. mark, where the lines built from south and north were finally to meet on 17th October 1943.

There was a coolie camp almost adjoining the POW working camp, Konkuita, and it was here that we were made to stay for a day. Again I should like to quote from Capt. Wild's report:

'Cholera broke out in the first POW camp early in May. This was directly attributable to the criminal negligence of the Japanese. For at Konkuita, the last staging-camp but two, every one of the thirteen marching parties was forced to camp, for one or more days within a few yards of huts filled with hundreds of cholera stricken coolies, on ground covered with infected faeces, where the air was black with flies. British officers asked for the loan of spades to remove this filth, but the

Japanese replied contemptuously, "use your hands".

'Lt.-Col. Harris protested vigorously to Lt.-Col. Banno, warning him of the inevitable consequences, and demanding that either all forward movement should be stopped or that the infection point should be by-passed. But nothing was done; the march forward continued, and by the end of May cholera was an epidemic in all five labour camps.'

There was little conversation between us as we 'marched', as all our concentration was centred on the effort of walking, and on helping and urging on the others. Wilkie and I moved up and down our Sappers in the column, trying to help and encourage where we could, but in certain places there was only room for us to walk in single file. Perhaps Wilkie and I weren't able to be together much on the march, but it was a relief to be able to talk at the end of the night's efforts.

At Nieke, 282 kms., the headquarters camp of 'F' Force, where Col. Banno of the IJA was in charge of POWs on this section of the railway, I believe we dropped off some of our numbers, but I am not sure about this. We also left men at Shimo Sonkurai before we finally reached our destination, Sonkurai Camp 2, after a march of 294 kilometres; and thus ended what has become known as the 'Death March'.

Sonkurai was the most northerly camp in Thailand, about five kilometres short of the Three Pagodas Pass, 299 kms., which marks the boundary between Thailand and Burma. It was one part of five labour camps, known as the Nieke Camps, along a 37-kilometre distance of railway track to be built. These camps were: Shimo Nieke, Nieke, Shimo Sonkurai, Sonkurai Camp 2 and Kami Sonkurai.

Geoffrey Pharaoh Adams has said that he was told, by a monk, the history of the Three Pagodas. They have been there for 300 years; the southern pagoda stands in Thailand, the central one actually marks the boundary, and the northern one is on Burmese soil.

The total length of the finished railway, from Nong Pladuk to Thanbyuzayat, was to measure 415 kms., the Burma teams completing 115 kms. coming south to the Three Pagodas Pass, 'F' Force completing 37 kms. from the

Three Pagodas Pass to Konkuita, and the remaining Thailand teams 263 kms., the Thailand section following the course of the Kwae Noi for its total length, except in certain parts where the mountainous country prevented this.

The working parties in Burma were mainly Australian, American, Dutch and Indian prisoners, plus a mixed unit of 500 British POWs from Sumatra under Capt. Dudley Apthorp, Royal Norfolks. The northern section of 152 kms., from Thanbyuzayat to Konkuita, came under the command of the 5th Railway Regiment, IJA, and the rest of the railway from Konkuita to Nong Pladuk was to be completed by the 9th Railway Regiment, IJA.

During the march we had discovered that there was not one word of truth in Major-General Arimura's undertakings which he had issued in Changi before the departure of 'F' Force. Our whole impression of the railway was one of shadows of sick and under-nourished men, working in their thousands at tasks far beyond human endurance, and we knew, now that we had arrived at Sonkurai, that this too would be our lot.

(iv) Sonkurai

We arrived at our camp at Sonkurai to find that it was merely a clearing in the dense jungle, in which were several long bamboo-framed huts, some with a semblance of an attap roof and others completely roofless. These huts had a central alleyway with a raised platform down each side of the hut. The platforms, made of split bamboo, were about two feet above the ground, and seven feet wide, and it was on these that we lived, slept and ate our morning and evening meals, such as they were. The width allotted to each man was about two feet, if he was lucky.

The camp was a sea of mud, as we were now at the height of the monsoon which was to continue without stopping for the next five months, and although we made a rule that no boots or footwear should be put on to the platforms in our huts, it was impossible to keep them clean. Bed bugs and lice were the others to share our living accommodation, as it had previously housed coolies, who weren't too particular about such things.

The sanitation was indescribable. The latrine pits were overflowing, because of the constant use and the now almost permanent rains, and the approach to them from the huts was fouled by men whose dysentery was so intense that they just could not reach the latrines in time.

Men were taken out on working parties as soon as they arrived, although we had only just completed six consecutive nights' marches, and were completely exhausted. We were given no rest.

The hours of work were excessive; 14 hours a day, with an hour for 'lunch' was a common occurrence, and work went on without a break for several months, with no consideration for the physical condition of the work force. For work purposes men were graded in three categories: .

1. Fit.
2. Fit for light duties in camp.
3. Excused all duties.

However, the Japanese engineers totally disregarded the health of the men, and the 'fit' and the 'fit for light duties in camp' men were taken out to do the really heavy work, and the 'excused all duties' men were made to do the fatigues around the camp.

The Japanese engineers were our complete masters, and were in no way controlled by the Camp Commandants, who were mostly junior NCOs. It was a pitiful sight each morning, as we were handed over to the engineers for the day and, in some cases, half the night as well. The engineers demanded a certain quota of workers each day, and this number always exceeded those who were not actually in 'hospital', and thus they would literally drive out, with sticks or weapons, men who were almost incapable of walking. A man with something to show, such as a blood-covered bandage round his leg, had a better chance of being excused work than a man dying of dysentery or malaria, although in some cases the Japanese engineers would kick the wound dressing to see if he screamed with pain, before excusing him work for the day.

The men never saw their camps in daylight, and so there was limited opportunity for personal hygiene. Washing in the river was stopped, owing to the scare of cholera, which was thought by most people to be a water-borne disease, and so men were unable to wash themselves or their clothes. It had been a practice of some of the coolies to dump their cholera dead in the river.

There were daily beatings of officers and men at work, sometimes even into unconsciousness. The object of these was to urge sick and weak men to physical efforts far beyond their remaining strength. Kicks and slaps were commonplace, and men were driven with wire whips and bamboo sticks throughout the day. If anyone worked badly, or appeared to be slacking, they were sometimes made to stand holding a rock or large piece of wood above their heads. If they let it drop, they were beaten. Otherwise, they had to stand at attention for hours and hours in the sun, but this didn't happen often because it was a waste of time, when they could have been working. Men were permanently shouted at: *Kora!* (Here you!), *Baka yaro!* (Fool!), and were forced to work, in the intense heat and pouring rain, at bayonet point, until they literally dropped in their tracks. The only Japanese words that were welcomed, were: *yasumi* (rest) and *meshi* (food), but, as can be imagined, these weren't uttered very often.

The five camps around Nieke, which 'F' Force occupied, the numbers of which were now down to 5,000 men, had been given the task of completing a stretch of 37 kilometres of railway, through hilly and flooded jungle just south of the Three Pagodas Pass. The work was arduous in the extreme, with men carrying logs far beyond their strength, and with many dozens of us standing for hours in waist-deep water, hauling on ropes with block and tackle. We were human pile-drivers.

The bridge we were constructing over the River Huai Ro Khi was a three-span wooden trestle-bridge, and small in comparison with some of those built lower down the line. It is strange that no bridge was actually built across the Kwae Noi, apart from two wooden bridges, Onte Bridge and Fukushima Bridge, built entirely by Japanese engineers, but spanned the tributaries of this great river on the eastern side. We were, of course, at the headwaters of the Kwae Noi, as we were only a few kilometres south of the Three Pagodas Pass, and it was in this district that the Kwae Noi started to flow.

When we were felling teak for the bridge, I suppose we were more fortunate than those men in some of the southern camps, in that the Japanese brought in elephants to help drag the timbers out of the jungle. I think that the sight of these great beasts and the complete understanding that existed between them and their mahouts, was the only thing of beauty that I can recall for almost the rest of my captivity. At night, after bathing the elephants in the river, the mahouts hobbled their forelegs and turned them free to forage. Obviously, with their heavy chains, they never wandered far, once they had found a good supply of food.

Some men, in their enthusiasm, tried to find colonies of white ants to embody in the building operations, in the hope that these would eventually destroy the timber joints, so weakening the bridge for the Japanese, but this proved to be a complete waste of time. There were no nuts and bolts, but iron spikes, driven in with heavy hammers, and building methods were extremely primitive, although, in spite of this, the bridges withstood the weight of the trains.

Where we were doing any levelling of the track, all materials had to be carried by hand in flat baskets, or on stretchers, as we had no such things as dumper trucks or even wheel-barrows. Our tools were few and simple and, if anyone slackened, they were goaded on at bayonet point by a Japanese engineer. If a man died at work, he had to be carried back to his camp to be counted at roll-call, before being allowed to be cremated or buried.

When we finished work in the evening, the only place to go was to our huts, where we lay in the dark on our bamboo platforms, and talked until sleep mercifully overtook us.

Our clothes were in a bad state. We tried to keep one pair of reasonably respectable shorts or long slacks, and so worked in our 'jap happys'. A jap happy was simply a loin cloth, and we lived and slept in these. On our feet we wore our klompers, or boots if they hadn't worn out; otherwise the bamboo splinters would have torn our feet. It was the cuts and bruises from bamboo that generally started tropical ulcers which, once they got a hold, were so difficult to cure without dressings. Many men developed poisoned feet, and 'trench foot' from continual work in the wet.

Lt.-Col. F. J. Dillon, OBE, MC (AA & QMG 18th Division), who was at my camp, Sonkurai, states that conditions were probably worse there than at any other camp, as the Engineer Officer, Lt. Abe, was conspicuous at all times in failing to stop brutal treatment by his men, even in his presence. He goes on to say, in his official report: 'Of the sixteen hundred men who went to Sonkurai camp in May, twelve hundred are dead and two hundred more are in hospital.' And all this within a few months. Lt. Abe was sentenced to death for his actions, in July 1947.

Unlike other POWs in Thailand, 'F' Force never came under the Thai administration, but remained under Major-General Arimura's headquarters at Changi. A part of the logistic troubles 'F' and 'H' Forces had was that the Japanese/Thailand administration had commandeered all the normal river trans- port and the Singapore administration had to make do with much deeper-draughted tugs and lighters from Bangkok. They could not freely navigate the river and at low water and at springtime it was impossible.

It became clear to us that, if the engineers continued to take all fit men and convalescent men to work every day, there would soon be no men at all, fit enough to work. They were, in fact, rapidly destroying their only available source of labour. The Japanese Administrative Headquarters at Nieke clearly agreed with this, but were quite unable to prevent the engineers carrying on with their catastrophic policy, and by the end of June this resulted in a mere 700 out of the original Force of 5,000 in the Nieke camps being able to work, and even these men were only fit for light duties.

The Japanese now drastically cut the rations of all the hospital patients, in the belief that this would drive men out to work in order to be given more food. This tactic might have worked in the case of malingerers, but malingerers do not die in their hundreds.

Many became desperately ill with cholera very quickly, as a direct result of the Konkuita incident, and were moved to another hospital hut we had built on the opposite side of the trace, under the care of a most dedicated doctor, L. H. Turner, R.A.M.C.. Many were dying daily but, apart from cholera, the swarms of mosquitoes caused malaria, both the benign and the cerebral malignant types; the latter sent men raving mad and subsequently killed them.

Tropical ulcers and pellagra were also grave problems, and the only method the doctors had of trying to deal with the ulcers was to scrape out the infected flesh with a sharpened spoon. The smell was nauseating and the screams were frightful. The Dutch doctors, on all parts of the railway, used to plant maggots in ulcers that wouldn't respond to treatment; these would eat away the putrified flesh, and thus prevent gangrene from setting in. Dressings were improvised from banana leaves, and bandages from torn off trouser legs, but some ulcers were so bad that limbs had to be amputated, usually with a saw. There were 70 amputations in all, but very few of the patients survived, not as a result of the amputation, but because they were undernourished and suffered from other diseases. These operations were carried out with very little anaesthetic, and under a mosquito net to try and keep away the myriads of flies.

The way the doctors worked under such appalling conditions was truly marvellous, and the one I remember with particular affection was Dr. Harry Silman, of 9th Battalion, Northumberland Fusiliers, who worked ceaselessly for the benefit of all. I had known him so well in Changi, as he was one of those with whom I had sat and talked on the roof of our barrack block at night. He was always cheerful, despite our circumstances, and he was to remain on the railway until he returned to Changi on 21st December 1943.

After the outbreak of cholera early in May, a Japanese medical party eventually arrived and 'glass rodded' us, to take a smear for analysis. This glass rodding was a somewhat crude method of finding out if any of us were cholera carriers. We were all paraded, coming forward in groups of 10 or so, to have a piece of glass rod pushed up our bottoms. By this time, men were dying in their dozens each day, mainly from cholera and dysentery.

(v) Cholera

Some days later, at about 1800 hours, the Japanese medical party returned, bringing with them a list of men who had been found to be carriers. I was the only officer, and I think my heart almost broke when my number was read out.

This piece of news did not surprise me, however, as I had most of the symptoms of cholera, but had not died in the 24 hours which seemed to be the normal period of survival. We were ordered to move out of camp immediately, and to form an isolation camp on the opposite side of the railway trace, near the hospital hut, about five or six hundred yards away. The senior officers appealed that at least the sick and dying should be left where they were until the following morning, but this was refused. All fit men turned out to help to carry and pitch some tents, brought up by the IJA medical party.

I shall never forget the torrential rain, which had been coming down virtually unceasingly for days, but as we moved across in the pitch dark, with all the sick, it seemed worse than ever. One report says there were 175 men, but I am convinced in my own mind that the number was nearer half that, but sadly many men died that night.

Next morning, as soon as it was light, I looked round our new sodden camp site, and was horrified to find it had been the cremation area for the coolies, and was littered with partly cremated bodies. Capt. P. U. Coates states in his diary, *Up Country with 'F' Force* that: 'This move was altogether the most inhuman thing I have ever witnessed'.

The hospital hut within our Area was now full to capacity with cholera patients and I, being the only officer identified as a carrier, was given the unenviable task of being put in charge of cremation. This is a part of my life I have never been able to forget and, indeed, I can hardly write about it. Each morning I would count the dead bodies outside the 'hospital', and again at midday. They looked deathly pale, with the light scattering of lime over them, which the Japanese had now provided as a means of trying to stop the spread of the disease. Cholera is an extremely painful disease with terrible contractions, vomiting, fast loss of weight due to complete dehydration, which in itself causes the skin to lose its elasticity, and men usually died in a sitting position, completely doubled up with pain. All these men had died in agony, and due to the unnatural contractions of their muscles, no man looked at peace, even in death.

But if I was sorry for myself and my fellow carriers, just think of the lives led by our doctors and their orderlies, who were in such intimate contact with their patients, knowing that there was so little they could do, and realizing full well the final consequence.

We spent most of the day cutting wood to build the pyres, and death came so quickly that men helping in the morning were themselves being cremated that same evening. It was frightful to see their charred and blackened bodies moving in the flames, as their muscles were affected by the heat.

Official figures show that 12 men were dying each day at Sonkurai. Although 750 men of 'F' Force died of cholera, by far the most deadly of all diseases was dysentery, aggravated by malnutrition, malaria and beri-beri, from all of which I suffered, but still only mildly from beri-beri.

As we could no longer work on the railway, the Japanese saw no reason why they should provide us with any rations. We were of no further use to them. We were kept alive solely on rice that the active men deducted from their own rations and, although the Japs knew that this was being brought over to us, they didn't stop it. In other words, they didn't want us to die, but saw no reason why we should live.

Lt.-Col. S. W. Harris must have been one of the most frustrated commanders of all time, in that he was completely unable to ensure that any of his written appeals for better conditions were ever passed to an authority higher than Lt.-Col. Banno, who was really quite useless. Nor could he gain access to the Regimental Commander of the Japanese Engineers, except on one occasion when, thank God, he was able to win his point. If he had failed in this, the result would have been one of the most inhuman acts in military history. Lt.-Col. Banno and his administration had already endorsed an order from the engineers for the immediate permanent expulsion of 700 desperately sick and dying men into the open jungle, in the worst of the monsoon rains, to make room for a native labour force.

After the War Crimes Trials in July 1947, Lt.-Col. Banno was sentenced to three years imprisonment, which seems somewhat lenient.

Lt.-Col. Dillon says, that in July:

'Several men, sometimes alone, sometimes in groups, disappeared into the jungle. Some probably had the idea of escaping, some undoubtedly only left so as to die in freedom, rather than in captivity, or disease and illness, also ill treatment. The men, on the whole, were in despair. The choice in front of them seemed to be death from disease, or never-ending toil and brutal treatment at the hands of the engineers. The prisoners' officers were unable to protect them in spite of all their efforts.'
He then refers to our escape attempt.

Again Capt. Wild says in his report:

'The attitude of the Japanese towards the sick was a mixture of callous indifference and active spite; for by their sickness they were regarded as impeding the Japanese war effort. Two remarks made, at official interviews, by Lt. Fukuda, Commander of one of the camps, will serve to illustrate this attitude:

"International Law and the Geneva Convention do not apply if they conflict with the interests of the Japanese Army."
'and again (to a senior Australian Medical Officer):

"You have in the past spoken somewhat boastfully of the Geneva Convention and humanity. You must remember that you are our prisoners of war, that you are in our power, and that under present circumstances these things do not apply." '

In the Sonkurai Area, and at Tanbaya 'Hospital' (so-called) in Burma, about 60 kilometres north of the Three Pagodas Pass, where many of our sick people were eventually taken in an effort to get them fit enough for the journey south after their section of the railway was finished, we lost a total of 83 Sappers.

Earlier on in this book, in the chapter on Changi, I wrote of
Padre Duckworth—what a great and caring person he was. He
came with us to Sonkurai and at the end of the war, on 12th
September 1945, he made a broadcast to London, entitled
Japanese Holiday. This was printed on board M.S. *Sobieski*, in the
Mediterranean Sea, on 18th October 1945, and, at the risk of
being somewhat repetitive, I would like to quote the whole of it:

"JAPANESE HOLIDAY"
A BROADCAST TO LONDON
by Padre J. N. Duckworth

The Japanese told us we were going to a health resort. We
were delighted. They told us to take pianos and gramophone records. *They* would supply the gramophones. We
were overjoyed and we took them. Dwindling rations and
a heavy toll of sickness were beginning to play on our
fraying nerves and emaciated bodies. It all seemed like a
bolt from the tedium of life behind barbed wire in Changi,
Singapore. They said: 'Send the sick. It will do them good.'
And we believed them, and so we took them all.

The first stage of the journey to this new found Japanese
Paradise was not quite so promising. Yes, they took our kit
and they took our bodies—the whole lot—in metal goods
wagons, 35 men per truck through Malaya's beating,
relentless sun for 5 days and 5 nights to Thailand, the land
of the *free*. For food, we had a small amount of rice and
some 'hogwash' called *stew*. We sat and sweated, fainted
and hoped. Then at Bampong station in Thailand they
said: 'All men go.' 'Marchee, marchee!' We said: 'What!
We're coming for a holiday.' They just laughed and in that
spiteful, derisive, scornful laugh which only a prisoner of
war in Japanese hands can understand, we knew that here
was another piece of Japanese buschido—deceit.

Our party marched, or rather dragged themselves for
17 weary nights, 220 miles through the jungles of Thailand. Sodden to the skin, up to our middles in mud, broken
in body, helping each other as best we could, we were still
undefeated in spirit. Night after night, each man nursed in

his heart the bitter anger of resentment. As we lay down in the open camps—clearings in the jungle, nothing more—we slept, dreaming of home and better things. As we ate boiled rice and drank onion water, we thought of eggs and bacon.

We arrived, 1680 strong at No. 2 Camp, Sonkurai, Thailand, which will stand out as the horror hell of Prison Camps. From this 1680 less than 250 survive today to tell its tale. Our accommodation consisted of bamboo huts without rooves. The monsoon had begun and the rain beat down. Work—slave work—piling earth and stones in little skips on to a railway embankment began immediately. It began at 5 o'clock in the morning and finished at 9 o'clock at night and even later than that. Exhausted, starved and benumbed in spirit we toiled because if we did not, we and our sick would starve. As it was the sick had half rations because the Japanese said 'No work, no food.'

Then came *cholera*. This turns a full-grown man into an emaciated skeleton overnight. 20, 30, 40, and 50 deaths were the order of the day. The medical kit we had brought could not come with us. We were told it *would* come on. It never did. We improvised bamboo holders for saline transfusions, and used boiled river water and common salt to put into the veins of the victims. Cholera raged. The Japanese still laughed and asked 'How many dead men?' We still had to work, and work harder. Presently, came dysentery and beri-beri—that dreaded disease bred of malnutrition and starvation. Tropical ulcers, diphtheria, mumps, small-pox, all added to the misery and squalor of the camp on the hillside where water flowed unceasingly through the huts at the bottom. A rising feeling of resentment against the Japanese, the weather and general living conditions coupled with the knowledge that their officers could do little or nothing about it, made life in the camp full of *dread* that each day would bring something worse. The lowest daily death rate came down to 17 only as late as September 1943, when the weather improved and things began to get a little better. Yet we had to work, there was no way out of it. Escape through the jungle as many gallant parties attempted, would only end in starvation and disease, and if the party survived and were eventually captured, the torture which followed was worse than death itself.

We were dragged out by the hair to go to work, beaten with bamboo poles and mocked at. We toiled, half-naked in the cold, unfriendly rain of Upper Thailand. We had no time to wash and if we did it meant Cholera. By day we never saw our bed spaces (on long platforms of those bleak hundred metre huts). Our comrades died, we could not honour them even at the graveside because we were still working.

The spirit of the jungle hovered over this Valley of the Shadow of Death and my boys used to ask me constantly: 'How long now Padre? What's the news?' We had the news. Capt. James Mudie, who now broadcasts from here, by an amazing piece of skill and resource, got it and gave it to us. And we lay and starved, suffered, hoped and prayed.

Never in my life have I seen such tragic gallantry as was shown by those men who lay on the bamboo slats and I speak now as a priest who ministered the last rites to all of them. Yet they died happy. Yes, happy to be released from pain, happy because our cause would not be suffered to fail among the nations of the earth.

No Medical Officers or orderlies ever had to contend with such fantastic, sickening, soul destroying conditions of human ailment. No body of men could have done better. We sank low in spirit, in sickness and in human conduct, but over that dark valley there rose the sun of hope which warned shrunken frames and wearied souls.

Here I would like to pay tribute to the stirling work and worth of some Officers amongst many to whom many men now living may owe their lives—Lt. Col. Andy Dillon, R.I.A.S.C., Lt. Col. John Huston, R.A.M.C., and to Lt. Col. Hutchison, MC, known affectionately to us as 'Hutch' also to Capt. E. J. Emery, who tended the sick even from his bedside and to Major Bruce Hunt of the Australian Imperial Forces. One cheering result comes from this dismal epoch in our lives, the coming close together in friendship and mutual understanding between the men of the United Kingdom and the men of Australia.

A new understanding has been born and will endure amongst those who think over the things which are of good report.

Those of us that came out of that hell, thank God for deliverance and for the memory of just men made perfect, whose examples as martyrs at the hands of the Japanese blaze yet another trail in the annals of human perseverance.

Singapore, 12th September 1945.

Printed on board M.S. *Sobieski*—in the Mediterranean Sea, 18th October, 1945.

ESCAPE

Chapter 6

ESCAPE

(i) Planning the Escape

WILKIE OFTEN made his way across to see me at night, knowing full well the risks he took, and the penalties had he been caught. However, once in my Area, the danger of being seen was reduced, as our guards were terrified of the cholera isolation camp and kept well away at all times. It was then that the question of escape arose, and here there is a divergence of opinion between Bill Anker and myself.

Bill, who was to be a member of our escape party, maintains that he, with Capt. Jack Feathers and Lt. J. F. Robinson, all members of 18th Division, R.A.S.C., had always been preparing for an escape since the early days of captivity, if and when the opportunity should arise. They had, therefore, been acquiring gradually, while on working parties in Singapore, water-purifying tablets and quinine as a prophylactic against malaria. They realized that, if an attempt to escape were to be started from Sonkurai, they would need a member with some sailing experience, and thus I was asked to join them, at Robinson's suggestion. He himself was a keen canoeist, and we had often talked in Changi of small boats and the water. I told him that Wilkie had far more experience than I, being a member of the Royal Ocean Racing Club, and so they decided to ask him too.

I certainly was unaware of this, and in any case was isolated from the others in the cholera camp, and so had little chance of talking with them. The first time the idea of escape was mentioned to me was by Wilkie, who felt that conditions prevailing in these railway camps should be brought to the notice of the outside world, which at that time was completely ignorant of conditions under which officers and men were living and working.

Obviously, Wilkie and I had also been thinking about the possibility of escape, otherwise I would never have risked keeping my collar stud compass or having my prismatic one built into my water bottle; and on reading the charges preferred against four of the survivors of our escape, it would appear that Wilkie was the prime mover.

It is not of great significance who originated the idea, but the important thing is that we ended up as one organized party, led by Wilkie. When he asked me whether I would join him, I thought our chances of success were remote but, on the other hand, knew that our chances of survival at Sonkurai were even more so; we had already lost a large proportion of our numbers through disease. It is the duty of an officer to attempt to escape but, this apart, the overriding factor which influenced my decision was that I had such a happy and loving family of my own at home and was determined, at any cost, to return to them again. The decision, therefore, was an easy one.

We started to plan the escape. There was no wire-netting round any of the camps, as the Japanese knew that the jungle alone was enough to deter any escape attempt and, of course, our skin colour was against us. We would have been recognized as prisoners as soon as we reached any populated area —there were large rewards for returning escaped prisoners— and so we ruled out the idea of trying to make our way north by the track running alongside the railway.

It was decided that an optimum number for the party should be eight to ten, although we knew that many people might have been anxious to join the escape, given the chance. The party had to be kept small; obviously the more who knew about it, the greater was the risk of discovery.

Bill Anker was a regular officer, a Captain in 18th Division, R.A.S.C., and we had known him since our trooping days, as he was in the *Mount Vernon* with us. He proved a tower of strength throughout the escape and, I am glad to say, survived and is alive today. He married a girl from my home village in Sussex, who went out to him in Malaya after the war, but sadly she died almost ten years ago. Bill was in charge of the rations at Sonkurai, and each day was able to put by a small amount of rice and a few tins of fish for us to take on the escape, which we kept in the isolation camp, where it was safe from Japanese eyes.

The two officers from Bill's Company joined us, of course. Both Jack Feathers and 'Robbie' Robinson had become friends of ours on the journey out from England. Jack was a cross-country Blue for either Oxford or Cambridge (I forget which university), and was married just before the war, but sadly he never knew that he had a son born during his captivity.

Robbie came from the Liverpool area. I remember he had some connections with Meccano, and told us that he was the child illustrated on the boxes of Meccano!

Ian Moffat was in the Royal Engineers, with the 9th Indian Division. He was a Lieutenant in Queen Victoria's Own Madras Sappers and Miners, and we had come to know him in Changi, where he had made a name for himself repairing watches. He came from the Argentine, where his family reared beef cattle. He survived the war and, as far as I know, returned to the Argentine.

Lt. Guy Machado, from the Straits Settlement Volunteer Force, was a Eurasian school teacher. Most units, on arrival in Singapore, had posted to them, as liaison officer, either a local member of the S.S.V.F. or the Malay Regiment, and this was how we came to know Guy. He was the one who brought our food across to the isolation camp each day, together with the small amount of uncooked rice and other food to build up our reserve for the escape. Guy survived the escape, and our subsequent recapture and deprivation, but sadly it had all been too much for him; he died in 1957 at the age of 50, and towards the end of his life he was plagued by memories of the escape. These played on his mind, and he sought the comfort of religion.

Lt. T. P. D. Jones of the Malay Regiment claimed to have some knowledge of the Burma coast. He also had a map of this area on a silk handkerchief and, although this could not be very accurate, we needed it badly. In fact, the advice we got from Jones, and others who said they had knowledge of the coastal region, proved to be highly inaccurate, but this was not their fault, as no-one had ever crossed from Sonkurai to the coast of Tavoy. They thought that we were probably about eighty kilometres from the coast, and from our knowledge of the jungle round the camp, and their knowledge of the coast, we calculated that this distance could be achieved in three weeks. How wrong we were! We had all underestimated the density of the jungle.

Cpl. Brown was an NCO in the Volunteers and a friend of Lt. Jones.

The tenth member of our party was an Indian fisherman, called Nur Mahommed. He came from Chittagong and had been taken prisoner by the Japanese when they had been moving south, earlier in the war. He was anxious to get home to his family, and we were glad to have him, as we thought he would prove a tremendous asset when we reached the coast. His knowledge of Urdu, and also his colour, would allow him to move about openly.

All those who joined our party did so on the understanding that, if anyone became a casualty during the escape, they would have to be left. It seemed a harsh decision, but we realized it was the only possible course of action, and each member verbally agreed to this.

Our aim was to reach a point on the coast near Ye. We hoped this might be achieved by meeting the Ye River, and then rafting down it to the coast. On reaching Ye we planned to obtain, by any means, a small sailing boat; this was where Nur Mahommed's help would be invaluable. We would then sail westwards, between the Delta of the Irrawaddy River and the northern tip of the Andaman Islands, and it was in this that Wilkie and I would be able to help. Wilkie was a very experienced yachtsman and, in fact, still owned an ocean racer which had been built for him while he was serving in Hong Kong before the war. I too had always been keen on sailing, having raced small boats when living in North Wales, so therefore had some knowledge to contribute to the escape.

Having estimated that we would need at least three weeks to cover these 80 kilometres, making a daily target of two and a half kilometres, which did not seem unreasonable at the time, we rationed our rice, allowing ourselves a few ounces a day. When the numbers were finally settled, we decided to leave in about ten days, having then been working on the railway for just over two months.

During these ten days I cut a way into the jungle until I came to a small river, the Huai Song Kalia, which appears to have been one of the headwaters of the Kwae Noi, so that when the day came to leave, we hoped to be well clear before our absence was reported or discovered. The Japanese would have heard us cutting through the jungle, had we not been able to get a clear start, but the sound of my cutting merely mingled with the sounds of those cutting wood for cremation. On coming to the river, our idea was to move either up or down, until we could find a well-disguised way into the jungle on the far bank, thus hopefully covering our tracks. This did, in fact, succeed.

Wilkie asked the senior Colonel at the camp, Lt.-Col. A. T. Hingston, R.A.O.C., to try and give us 24 hours' start before reporting our absence. However, we were unfortunate in that the day we left happened to coincide with one of the surprise parades before the Japanese, where numbers were physically counted, and thus our absence was discovered within a few hours of leaving. I learnt later, from some of the survivors who returned from Sonkurai, that the Japs immediately started a search of the camp surroundings, but that this was a half-hearted affair, as they presumably thought we would have no chance of survival in the jungle.

I also learnt, unofficially, that Lt.-Col. Hingston was threatened with execution, but that he was let off the hook. However, I can find no trace of this threat in any of the official reports.

In any event, the Japanese did not pick up our trail, and the escape began as planned.

(ii) Break-out

On 5th July 1943, just before first light, Wilkie and the other members of the party came across, one at a time, to my cholera isolation camp. If one man had been discovered leaving the main camp, it would have been up to him to extricate himself from his immediate predicament without involving the others, and the escape attempt would have carried on without him. If they had all been caught leaving their Area in a group, the whole attempt would have been jeopardized.

I think none of us had slept during the night; I know I certainly hadn't. I had committed myself to the escape attempt and, in a way, was anxious to get started, because at that time we still had hope, but little idea of what lay ahead.

I felt that, if I stayed in camp, I might possibly live, but the chance was remote. If we failed in the escape, there were the two alternatives: death from some accident or starvation in the jungle or, if we were recaptured, death at the hands of our enemies, and pray God this would be by firing squad and not by the two-handed Samurai sword. These were the thoughts that went through my mind during that last night in the camp. Without doubt, I had taken the greatest decision of my life. We had to succeed.

We had accumulated about seventy pounds of rice, some soya beans, dried fish, whitebait, chillies and a few tins of fish. This would allow us about four ounces of rice daily, supplemented by additional flavouring, for about four weeks. We anticipated reaching the coast in three weeks, but reckoned we could survive for an additional week on these meagre rations.

In each pack we carried some form of blanket and ground sheet, and our share of the communal rations, plus the following items:

> Prophylactic quinine, to be taken nightly; mosquito cream; water purifying tablets; rope; string; candles; matches; mugs; billycans.

Between us we carried one axe, three parangs, one or two lighters and a spare compass or two.

Each of us carried a haversack, probably an old gas-mask container, or something of that size. In these we took our own personal possessions, including any spare clothing, and in my case I still had the two photographs of Lindsay and Roger which I had received in Changi. These, with my travellers' cheques and some notes on celestial navigation, I kept dry in a piece of old ground sheet.

Ian Moffat carried his share of our communal load in one pack, plus an extra pack full of his own things, including, I remember, a pack of cards and a tin of talcum powder, with which he used to dust his items of especial value or interest. Everything was meticulously wrapped in pieces of gas cape.

When I had first equipped myself in Liverpool, I had bought a Jaeger sleeping-bag which was, in fact, an ordinary sleeping-bag but made with three thicknesses of blanket, so that theoretically one could have either one or two coverings on top; one thickness had long since been sacrificed on the march up from Ban Pong, because of the weight. I now cut a twelve-inch strip from the top, to form a 'cholera belt', and bound it, as a permanency, round my middle to keep it warm.

I had two small tropical ulcers on my legs, but Capt. Harry Silman, R.A.M.C., who was with us in Sonkurai, had given me two M & B 693 tablets, the early sulphonamides, which I put into each ulcer, binding them up with a piece of mosquito netting.

We were all wearing khaki drill long trousers, with the bottoms tucked into our socks or bound round with a form of short puttee, in the hope of keeping out as many leeches as possible. My most treasured possessions were my Lotus Veltschöen boots, which I had rarely used since the fall of Singapore, except on the march, as in Changi I had worn my home-made klompers or gone around barefoot.

Before setting out from the camp, I had broken open my water-bottle, in order to recover my compass, but I had been able to replace the bottle quite easily, as so many were left by those who had died of cholera. Of course, I still had my collar stud compass, held in reserve.

We had no goodbyes to say, as we had tried to keep our departure secret, and I felt it better that no-one in my cholera camp should know anything about it, in case they were questioned after we had gone. Even though I knew this was unlikely, as the Japanese were terrified to come near the cholera carriers, I felt it was safer to put no-one at risk.

We started by making our way along the track I had already cut, until we came to the Huai Song Kalia, which by now had become a roaring torrent, following the recent heavy storms. When I had last seen it a few days before, it would have been simple to make our way upriver, walking in the water. We could not afford to leave any track on the bank that the Japanese might follow, so there was nothing for it but to forge upriver against the current, until we found a slightly less dense patch of undergrowth.

Having achieved this, we left the water, realizing thankfully that our tracks had been well and truly covered by the high level of the river. We set our hopeful course to the west, to which we determined to hold irrespective of whatever hazards might stand in our way, but little did we know that the Taungnyo range of mountains ran in an unbroken line south from Moulmein, and that we had to cross them in order to keep to our route to the coast.

During the first few days after we left Sonkurai we made reasonable headway, as the jungle was not too bad compared with that which we were to meet later. We were able to cover about four kilometres a day, which was almost within our projected schedule.

I couldn't help thinking of my family at home at this time. 9th July was Roger's fifth birthday, and I had already missed nearly two years of his childhood; I thought of the birthday cake and candles, and felt that Lindsay was wondering, as I was, whether I should ever join them again at Roger's birthday celebrations.

Our routine varied little from day to day. Our morning meal was similar to the breakfasts that we had endured since Singapore fell. This comprised a small helping of soggy boiled rice, known by all as 'pap', and our drink was now boiled water, and from this we filled our water bottles for the day.

We always had an advance party of three; two with parangs trying to slash a track, and the third watching the compass, hoping to keep to a permanent westward course, towards the setting sun.

About midday we would rest for a short time, but could not afford any more food until the evening. After our short break, we would set off again with changed leaders, as constant slashing with the parangs really took it out of us, and particularly in those places where we came across old tall bamboos which had fallen and become interlocked, and at such a height that in no way were we able to climb over them.

We would normally give up by about five o'clock, if we were in an area where we could cut bamboo poles to erect a shelter for the night. At first we were rather ambitious and made a platform about one foot above the ground, with a roof above that would provide sitting headroom. The roof was normally made of any branches with leaves attached. While some were making the shelter, others were collecting wood to make a fire for cooking, and attempting to dry our blankets. We usually managed to keep this fire going all night, so that we should have a source of heat to cook our rice next morning, and to ward off any wild animals that might approach too near.

We had been warned of tigers in this part of the country, and we also knew this was an area inhabited by small herds of Asian elephants who, with their natural dislike of bright sunlight, kept to the denser parts of the jungle.

Once the fire was burning, it was comparatively easy to keep it going, but it was always difficult to kindle, as the jungle wood was permanently damp. It was perpetually raining and, with the intense humidity, the jungle was a steaming mass of choking bamboo and green vegetation, through which we were fighting our way. So far so good; the Japs hadn't found our tracks.

The highlight of our food was when we found a turtle in a stream, during this early part of the escape. We didn't really know how to kill it, but we managed to overcome this obstacle, baked it on our fire, and it made a good and sustaining meal.

A constant source of worry to us was not the fear of the wild animals or snakes, but the fear of leeches. Whatever precautions we took, they always managed to get through to our bodies and, once they had attached themselves to us, it was difficult to get rid of them. They clung to our necks, got up our sleeves, and we never realized they were there until we happened to touch that spot and felt the awful lump, as large as a grape, full of blood. If the heads were not removed from our skins, bleeding would ensue and continue without stopping, and so we tried to burn them off with the embers from our fire. To this day, leeches are one of the most loathsome things in the world, as far as I am concerned, although of course, I have never seen them since.

I will now use the notes that we made together in Changi Gaol in 1944, after our trial, as a guide. These notes were written in pencil on odd scraps of paper, and I remember I mentioned no names, but just initials, in case the Japs confiscated the notes and punished those whose names were written in them. It is amazing that they have survived to be helpful to me now; it must have been in our minds at the time that a book should eventually be written about our escape.

'On 18th July Robinson's hand became poisoned and was soon festering badly.' This could have started from a bamboo scratch, which was one way ulcers started, or it could have been caused by the use of the parang. The constant slashing with this tool opened up all the joints in our fingers.

'We soon ran into more hilly country', and later the jungle became so dense that literally hundreds of bamboos, four to five inches in diameter, which had fallen down after their natural span of life, formed an impenetrable interlocking barrier. In places such as this, we were lucky if we managed to go more than half a kilometre in the day, as we were trying to haul ourselves up steep hills and slash at the same time. This was the most difficult terrain we had yet come across, and we were all feeling the strain.

All the energy needed for this constant cutting, coupled with our very meagre supply of food, caused us to get weaker and weaker and, after struggling for three weeks, we could see very little hope of reaching the coast. Sleep was hard to come by in these uncomfortable conditions, and we were probably beyond sleep anyway, being far too exhausted.

At night, I just lay thinking of the past, realizing what a happy life I had lived and how fortunate I had always been. Perhaps at the time, I had taken this for granted, but I knew now that I would never again accept anything as being my right. There was only one thing I wanted, and that was my family, with a small home, no matter how humble. This was my driving force.

It was just about this time that I was convinced I heard the horn of a motor car. I told the others about this, but none of them had heard anything, and it later transpired that we were at least 40 to 50 kilometres from a road. It must have been a figment of my imagination, but to this day I can still clearly hear that horn.

Predominant among the sounds of the jungle was the chatter of the monkeys. We saw many of them up in the trees, but of course could never get near enough to catch one for food, and they used to rush about the tree tops with great agility and speed. We had to keep a constant look-out for the small deadly black tree snakes, about which we had been warned when cutting wood for the bridge we were building on the railway at Sonkurai. This was an added hazard, and we could well have done without it.

As far as food was concerned, we always hoped that we might find edible berries, but never did so. On one occasion we found a wild banana tree, but there was very little eatable fruit on the bananas, as each one had a huge core of black pips. Sometimes we came across fungi growing on the trees, and I ate this, working on the assumption that anything that was poisonous would make me sick immediately. I should add that ever since I became a cholera carrier in the camp at Sonkurai, and coupled with my dysentery, anything I ate went straight through me, and this continued now.

We cut down on our rations even more and on: '*25th July we were down to our last rice and three days later we shared one small tin of pilchards between the ten of us*'.

(iii) Five Men Die

'*On 29th July we suffered our first casualty. Cpl. Brown could not be found on awakening in the morning.*' For the last few days he had been very ill with tropical ulcers, particularly on his back, and gangrene had set in. He had warned us on several occasions that he was quite unable to carry on, and at times became delirious. However, he must have had great courage to 'walk out', instead of being a liability to us.

As the nights were so cold and wet, we were all getting up at frequent intervals to relieve ourselves or to stoke the fire, and so no-one worried if someone was moving about. The only way Brown could have gone was back along the track we had cut, and we searched for him for a while; indeed, it would have been heartless not to have done so, but we did not dare to waste too much of our dwindling energy and time in retracing our steps, and so it was then that we had to implement our terrible agreement, and to go on without him.

At night we now made a simple shelter, for we no longer had the strength to do more than rig up some form of cover in an attempt to keep off the ever persistent rain, and to try and make a bed of leaves or twigs. Previously, our conversation had been hopeful, but after losing Brown we were all too sad to say much, for we knew in our hearts that this was not an isolated case but rather something we should inevitably have to face again. Which one of us would be the next to die?

'*30th July; Recce. party down to two. Bradley sprained wrist and unable to use parang. Anker cut thumb on right hand, thus he also unable to cut.*'

'*2nd August; Jack Feathers died during night.*' Poor Jack, he was very thin and troubled by swollen feet. His wife had been expecting their first baby when the Division left England in the autumn of 1941, and Jack never knew that he had a son, and of course he never saw his child. He was a wonderful person and we had all become very fond of him when trooping, and later in Changi. He worried a lot on the escape, not knowing how his wife was. I met her once after our return to England.

'*5th August; Wilkie died shortly after making camp in the evening, presumably from heart failure, as we had just encountered some of the steepest gradients of our journey.*' For the last few days he had been suffering from terrible pains in the region of his heart, and being normally such a large heavy man, the excessive loss of weight just proved too much for him, and he was completely exhausted. I felt this loss more than any other, as he had always been such a true friend to me. He was a fine man, and I am proud to have known him so well. Had he not died that night, I think I would have stayed with him, if I had had the courage, as I felt that I too could not go on much longer because I was also getting severe pains round my heart. However, I still held on to my overriding goal, which was to see my family again. Thank goodness it was during the night that he had died, and so the question of my staying with him did not arise. It was desperately hard to carry on without Wilkie, but it would have taken a brave man to tell the others to go on, and to wait alone with him for death in the jungle.

What amazed me was the strength of will shown by Jack, Wilkie and later Robbie. They literally pushed on with the escape until they reached our night's camp, when they just lay down, exhausted, and died.

By now our blankets, which were permanently wet because of the incessant rain, were becoming a tremendous burden to carry, and we used to try to wring them out at night. It was hard to keep our matches dry, but for as long as they lasted, or our lighters worked, we were able to make a fire each evening, and to take turns to hold our blankets over the flames. We never managed to dry them, but at least we were making an effort to do so, and warming ourselves in the process. Sometimes at night, not only were we lying under damp blankets, but we were now actually lying down in water. It was quite impossible to find anywhere dry, and as a result we were all now suffering from trench feet and ulcers. Our boots and groundsheets had rotted, due to being constantly soaked.

By this time Ian Moffat's legs were completely covered with ulcers, from his thighs to his feet, but still he kept going on with the struggle, even though he must have been in almost unbearable pain. At night, the smell of these ulcers was nauseating.

Even when we were on what appeared to be the top of a hill, we could get no clear view forward to see if there was any easier way to go, because the jungle still hemmed us in so closely. We were forced to keep on going, never deviating from our westward compass course.

'*9th August; Jones was missing from our evening camp site for two hours, but after searching back along our track, we found him unconscious. For the next two days we almost carried Jones, and finally came to a tributary of the River Ye, for which we had been aiming. There we found an old hut, which had been used by deer hunters, and of course we occupied this for our night's camp. It was in this hut that Robbie died from septicaemia and dysentery;'* he had never recovered from the poisoning of his hand in the early days of our escape. He too had been a great friend in Changi, and I felt his death deeply.

'*That same night Jones, who had been suffering from dysentery from the start, and thus had not been allowed to carry any foodstuffs, begged us to carry on next morning and leave him behind, as he was virtually unable to move.*' Thus the only course open to us was to try and make him as comfortable as possible, and to leave him with a full water bottle. And so we said goodbye to a very brave man, knowing that no-one would ever see him alive again. '*We told him we would send help if we should reach any habitation within forty-eight hours.*'

We had set out as a party of ten, and we were now reduced to five. We had been working our way for approximately six weeks, and for the last two weeks had had nothing to eat at all. The one thing we didn't lack was water to drink, and this we either scooped out of puddles, or caught the rain in our mugs. We could now hardly sleep at all at night, as most of us had badly bruised hips and backs, and our blankets and kit had to remain wet, as we could no longer wring them out, being too weak. The mosquitoes were a constant worry, as of course we had no nets, and to this day the sound of a mosquito in a room worries me terribly.

(iv) The Raft

'*14th to 17th August; we arrived at the Ye River*', a wonderful slow-moving one and the one for which we had been aiming. It was here that we had our first unobstructed view of the sky since we left Sonkurai, and we decided that our best course of action was to stay on the bank of the river and build a raft. We realized that once we were rafting, there would be no possible chance of hiding if we should be seen by any human beings, which was a possibility as we were obviously near the lower lands on the coast. However, we were not worried about this, as we must have been very near the end of our stamina and would have perished anyway. The fact that we might be shot or recaptured was something we would almost have welcomed.

'*We camped on the right bank for three days while we cut bamboo and made a raft*', using strips of our blankets to bind the poles together. We were all teribly weak, and anything we did took a much longer time than it would normally have done. We were unable to walk more than a few yards at a time.

I see on the notes that I again made reference to Ian Moffat's ulcers, they were full of maggots, and it was probably due to these that his legs were saved, as they devoured the putrified suppurating flesh, thus preventing gangrene. I am sure both legs would have been amputated under normal conditions.

In the notes Moffat writes: '*Bradley and Machado fainting regularly throughout the day, and Anker can only use left hand. Nur Mahommed very weak.*' Bill Anker also adds that: '*Jones' previous knowledge of the country had proved wrong, giving rise to the expectation of reaching the coast in three weeks, and thus the lack of food.*' We had now had no food since 28th July 1943.

'*17th August; we launched the raft and set off down what appeared to be an ideal wide, slow-moving river*', and I think that we now felt slightly more relaxed at the thought of not having to cut a track with the one remaining serviceable parang, and knowing that we must reach the coast or human habitation within a few days.

However, this situation wasn't to last for long, because: '*the river suddenly turned west and we were horrified to see a narrow gorge in front of us. We had run into rapids, the first three of which we successfully negotiated, but our raft broke up on the fourth*', totally unable to withstand the force of this cauldron of swirling water. There was nothing we could have done to prevent our flimsy raft being smashed up completely, and as a result of this disaster we lost our packs in the river, and Moffat his boots, which had been hanging round his neck by their laces. However, we managed to save our haversacks, in which were our few personal possessions.

Moffat, Machado and I swam to the bank, and Bill Anker, and Nur Mahommed held on to parts of the raft and drifted into the side. The three of us who had swum ashore, made our way along the bank, hoping to find the other two, and luckily they had both been washed up on our side of the river.

We now had no means of cutting through the jungle, having lost our parang, although here it was not so dense. We had no blankets and were now in a much worse position than before we had started to build the raft.

(v) Kampongs Karni and Arkan

'That day we saw our first human beings since escaping. They were two Burmese hunters, who were making their way up the bank of the river. They took us to their shack where they gave us some food, the first for so long, and there we spent the night. We tried to persuade them to search for Jones, but to no avail, but by then he must have died.' Nur Mahommed was very helpful to us at this time, because he could, more or less, understand the dialect of these people, and through him we were able to communicate with them.

'The next day, 18th August, the hunters led us to Karni, a small kampong (village), where we met the Headman.' We were as elated as it was possible to feel in our weak condition, and we dared to hope that success and freedom were within our grasp. The Headman appeared to be helpful to us, although later we were convinced that it was he who had been instrumental in getting us arrested.

We had, in fact, almost achieved the first stage of our ambition, as we were on the coastal plain within a few miles of Ye, which had always been our target. For me this was especially gratifying, as it was I who had set the compass course for most of the way.

The Headman, apparently, had very little food, or else he was not prepared to waste any of it on us! However, he did give us two bananas each. He could speak very little English, although he had been in the Burmese Army at some time, and delighted in showing us how he used to slope arms, order arms and present arms!

His house was a little wooden one-roomed shack, raised up on stilts. It was roofed with attap, and stood in a small clearing on the edge of the kampong. To be fair to him, I think the kampong had very little food, and the villagers were living off their own fruit and vegetables, and a small amount of rice.

As dusk fell, he allowed us to sit on the veranda of his house, and we talked for most of the evening, under a beautiful starlit sky. His fair young wife joined us on the veranda, and this was the first girl we had seen for nearly two years! She really was a most beautiful creature, sitting there quite naturally in her brightly-coloured sarong, and completely bare above the waist. Even in our emaciated state, we were not unappreciative of her beautiful breasts.

We spent the remainder of the night lying on the ground under the Headman's house, thinking how incredible it was that we had almost achieved our goal, and that whatever befell us now, we would not suffer the same terrible deaths as those of our party who had died in the jungle, nor should we die alone.

'*19th August; we were taken to a shack, where we met the Headman of Arkan, another kampong nearby, and two of his satellites.*' He was keen to take our money to buy us eggs and tobacco, etc., but these did not materialize.

'*20th August; we were moved to Arkan, Bill Anker, Nur Mahommed and myself on foot, and Machado and Moffat by river, as Moffat's legs were so bad, and Machado was very weak indeed and found walking difficult.*' We were warmly welcomed by the inhabitants of Arkan, who showered us with gifts of fruit, which was probably very bad for us in our condition at the time. The generosity of these people and their happy smiling faces has always remained with me, as kindness such as this was something we had not encountered for so long.

'*Later we were taken to "Burma House", a disused Police Station, and after that to a Burmese home*', where two young men and their wives lived; again we sat on the veranda outside. One of the men asked us whether we would like a chicken curry, which of course was accepted, and I shall never forget him getting out his muzzle-loading gun, sitting down cross-legged on the floor next to us to prime it, and then disappearing round the back of the house. There followed a tremendous report, and he returned, full of smiles, carrying a scraggy chicken for us to see, which he plucked immediately.

While his wife was cooking the curry, we went down to the river and stripped off completely for a good wash, a thing we had not done for weeks, not daring to take off our now completely rotten boots. We must have been an unedifying spectacle, to say the least, but the people of the kampong seemed to enjoy it, and sat on the bank watching and laughing. They appeared to be happy and apparently well nourished by the food they grew themselves, and looked attractive in their multi-coloured sarongs and loin cloths.

After our wash, we went back for our memorable chicken curry. We ate far more than we should have done, as it was the first real food we had seen for so long, and it seemed strange to think that the chicken had been running about just an hour and a half beforehand.

It was only later, after the end of the war, that I found how little I could eat at any one time, and even now I do not have a very large appetite.

We had felt, ever since meeting the Headman of Karni, that we had been sold, and Nur Mahommed had been worried, at the time, about staying in the kampong. He communicated his fears to us, and we talked about trying to leave the village, but we realized that we were constantly watched and had probably already been sold to the IJA. In any case, I think that Bill Anker was the only one of us left with enough strength to attempt to move on.

After the war, the Headman of Karni was taken and tried for war crimes, his crime being that of selling escapees. It was Col. Wild, to whom we owe so much, who, in his capacity as War Crimes Liaison Officer, was to go up to Burma and have him arrested.

ARREST AND TRIAL

Chapter 7

ARREST AND TRIAL

(i) Prisoners Again

WE WERE AWARE that we were never left unwatched, and were almost certain that we had been either reported or sold to the Japanese. Sure enough, the next day: *'21st August; a unit of Japanese troops arrived, and we were under arrest. They were, in fact, two Japanese soldiers, who were accompanied by a Burmese Police Inspector and three policemen.'*

Our hearts sank. Obviously we were extremely worried at falling into Japanese hands again, and had no idea what our future might hold, bearing in mind the fact that earlier, in Selarang, we had been forced to sign a form accepting death as the punishment for an attempted escape. We had no idea whether we would be tried before a court, or whether we would be executed there and then. I was exhausted, both physically and mentally, and I don't think I was able to take in the gravity of the situation, beyond the feeling of fear. They had no interpreter with them, and only knew a few words of English, but the main thing in which they appeared to be interested was to find out from where we had come. This led us to think that we would probably be taken for official questioning, before any drastic action was taken.

They confiscated our money and few belongings, including any letters and photographs of our families and children that we had managed to keep. These they put in a small tin box. Each time our possessions were taken from us, the Japs were most meticulous about looking after them and passing them on to any new guards who might take us over.

Still wearing the only clothes we possessed, but perhaps looking a little cleaner after our bathing: *'we went down to the river and were taken to Ye by boat. Here we were housed* in the Japanese Headquarters, which had formerly been the Ye General Hospital. *We remained in this building for three days until 24th August, and were individually interrogated by an IJA Sergeant Major at various intervals during the day'*, but this was civilized questioning, and very unlike some of our later interrogation by the Japanese Kempei-Tai. In our notes I see that Bill Anker says we were given coffee and biscuits by our investigators.

'On 24th August we were taken by the Japanese Kempei-Tai to Moulmein, travelling second class on the train from Ye', a journey of about 140 kilometres. On our arrival at the station there was already a train waiting, and our guards took over two adjoining compartments, each one having its own lavatory. Two of us were locked in one lavatory and three in the other; these small cubicles were absolutely filthy and evil smelling, with stale water lying on the floor.

It seemed a characteristic of most of our Japanese guards to assert their authority by shouting and generally knocking us about, and then later to relent and become more amenable. On this occasion they eventually allowed us out of the lava-tories, and let us sit with them in the compartment, where they enjoyed looking at our photographs, particularly those of our children. Before we reached Moulmein we actually managed to borrow some money from them with which to buy a cup of coffee at one of the stations! I cannot under-stand why they could not let us use some of our own money, but perhaps they had already made a note of how much we each had when they confiscated our belongings.

We all had a certain amount of money with us, because before setting out on the escape we had sold anything that was saleable, in order to have funds with which to buy an old sailing boat. For this I had let go my Rolex Oyster wrist-watch.

When we left the train at Moulmein we understood that we were being taken to a hospital, but in fact: *'we were taken to the Military Police Headquarters, where we spent the night; that is, all of us except Moffat, who was taken to a hospital cell, No. 13 at the Civilian Gaol, because the Japanese simply could not stand the smell of his suppurating ulcers.'* The re-mainder of us were put in a cage-like cell with other prisoners, and at feeding times a communal round brass dish of rice, about two feet in diameter, was left on the floor, from which all prisoners helped themselves with their fingers.

'*The following day, 25th August, we were again interrogated by the Kempei-Tai, and then taken over to the Civilian Gaol.*' Our Japanese guard banged on the gates of the Gaol until we were admitted and taken before the Chief Jailer, whose reception led us to believe we were in for a hard time with him.

He signed what I believe was a receipt for us and our personal belongings, after which the Japanese guard left the gaol. The Chief Jailer immediately stood to attention and saluted us, apologizing for his rough reception which he thought was necessary if we were to be left in his charge.

I think it was after two days that: '*it was decided we should be put into what had been the hospital wing*'. This was a large room, about 25 feet square, with barred windows on three sides, starting at floor level. Although the room was completely bare, it was clean and bright with whitewashed walls.

'*A Sikh doctor, Sohan Singh, MD, BS (Rangoon), came to see us, but he had almost no drugs.*' He was horrified by our condition, and insisted that our diet should include dhal, which is like a split lentil. We all had tropical ulcers, to a greater or lesser degree, Ian Moffat's being far worse than anyone else's.

We were weighed by Dr. Singh, and my weight was just under six stone. I had dysentery extremely badly by now, and we all suffered, at various intervals, from malaria; we had had no nets to protect us from the mosquitoes on our escape. As far as I remember, the only medicine Dr. Singh had was some aspirin, but he would not allow me any, because he was worried by my heart. I must say, he did all he could for us, and even found makeshift beds for us. These were wooden frames and legs with interwoven string as mattresses, and they certainly made a welcome change from lying on bare concrete, or the rain-soaked floor of the jungle.

Dr. Singh had no bandages, but tore up turbans and any other material he could lay his hands on to bind up Moffat's legs, which by now were simply frightful. I don't think I have ever seen worse wounds.

I cannot say enough in gratitude to Dr. Singh, and the Chief Jailer and his assistants, for all that they tried to do for us, with their almost non-existent resources. They found towels and soap, and even toothbrushes — luxuries we had not known for ages, although when in Changi we used to scrub our teeth with coconut husks. We had some money, but the Japanese had made the Chief Jailer sign for it, and so he was unable to use any on our behalf.

The windows of our ward looked out into the prison yards, and during the daytime dozens of prisoners sat silently round our windows, just staring in at us. We used to wonder what they were thinking about, as their faces looked so completely blank.

In a cell on the opposite side of the courtyard was a Burman, apparently mad, and he called out to us by day and night. He had some knowledge of English, but it was difficult to understand what he was saying. Dr. Singh told us that he came from a wealthy local family, and that he was rashly promising to get us all the food we needed. This was, of course, not possible and only a figment of his imagination.

We were given two adequate meals of rice and dhal daily, and really felt that if we could only be allowed to remain here we should certainly survive. However, this was not to be, and on: '*5th September, after about twelve days, Lt. Fukuda and three guards arrived and took us, with some Dutch POWs, to a wayside camp south of Moulmein*', possibly Kami Sonkurai, with the idea of taking us down the railway to Thailand.

We travelled by lorry, and the journey was along a very rough track beside the railway. We were bounced about in the back of this truck, and as we had no flesh on us to soften the bumps, the pain was really quite awful. At one time sirens sounded, the lorry stopped with a jolt, and all our guards vanished, but there was nothing we could do but wait for the 'all clear', as we had no chance of escaping again in what was now a populated area, where our colour would have betrayed us immediately. In spite of this air-raid warning we saw no planes.

The wayside camp to which we came was another railway camp, near the northern end of the line. *'We were now separated from Nur Mahommed'*, and were never again to be reunited with him during the war, although we heard that he was eventually taken down to Outram Road Gaol in Singapore.

Capt. T. Wilson, R.A.M.C. (now Professor Wilson) had been detailed to accompany 'F' Force as an adviser on antimalarial work and nutrition. He kept a diary and while at Kami Sonkurai made the following entry:

'Friday 10th September: Items of interest have been a surprise kit inspection by the Nips, when jack knives were confiscated, a threat of starvation for whole camp because a pick was missing, and the arrival of the recaptured prisoners, who escaped from No. 2 camp at end of June. Five have died and four officers and one Indian brought back. In pretty bad shape, one with legs covered with ulcers, which we are allowed to dress daily. Following interrogation, are dieted now on a ball of rice and salt twice a day, plus water. No news of their ultimate fate.'

'On 7th September we were moved to a Japanese camp, where the four of us were made to sit in a line, cross-legged, with a bamboo pole lashed to our wrists behind our backs.' The Japanese Captain tried to kick in Machado's teeth with the wooden clogs he was wearing and, being trussed so tightly, Machado was unable to take any avoiding action. Later that evening another officer ordered that we should be released and allowed to lie on the ground for the night, and we were given two rice balls each.

Perhaps the only comfort was the fact that the guards kept a good fire going all night, so that they themselves could keep warm, and by its light they were able to keep an eye on us. This fire kept us warm, too, of course.

(ii) Back to the Railway

'8th September, 1943: we were moved on to Thanbyuzayat', a large camp about 60 kilometres south of Moulmein, and the Japanese administrative terminus for the northern section of the railway in Burma. A point of interest is that the name Thanbyuzayat means 'little resting place', and was so named

by a Buddhist many years ago. The first POWs had arrived here at the end of September 1942, and established a base camp and hospital but, because of the Allied raids, the camp was evacuated in June 1943, and the POWs, including the sick, were sent to other camps. However, it was in use again now.

Thanbyuzayat was a little resting place for us, too. As events transpired, it almost became our permanent 'resting place'. *'We remained here for two weeks in a small leaky bamboo hut at the rear of the Japanese quarters, in which we had just enough room for the four of us to lie down. Every night we were handcuffed together, Machado to Moffat, and myself to Anker. Our guards were now Koreans, under Nakamura'*, and these guards were much taller than the Japanese. I don't think they were prepared to try and understand anything we said, whereas the Japanese would at least try to do so, but we generally managed to convey our meaning to them by odd words and gesticulations.

I remember it was here that we first discovered lice on the remains of our blankets, and we must have spent hours trying to rid ourselves of these. Having lost our original blankets on the escape, by using them to make our raft, these must have been some given to us in Moulmein Gaol.

'Captain Toyama told us that we were to be executed at this camp', a piece of information that didn't surprise us and, because of this, for the first two days the food was good. It came from the Japanese cookhouse and even contained meat with the rice and vegetables, and we were also given weak tea. We were even allowed medical attention, but on the second day this was again refused.

'Cholera was present in the camp, and men in the cholera isolation camp, either carriers or some of the few who had made a temporary recovery, were forced to cut wood to build a pyre on which to cremate us. These men were under a Captain Knowles.'

'It was here that we had our hardest and most prolonged interrogation, by Col. Banno, who was stationed at Nieke, the Administration Headquarters for 'F' Force, a Kempei-Tai Sergeant-Major, and Mr. Sangi.' This lasted, on and off, for

most of our stay here. The Kempei-Tai Sergeant-Major kept a leather belt on his table at all times, and did not hesitate to use it in order to try and extract information. We each had to make a written statement about what information we would have passed to the British forces had we succeeded in our escape.

My written account was brief. I said that, as we had been put into closed metal rice trucks for the journey up through Malaya to Ban Pong, we had seen little of the country and, as we had marched from Ban Pong up to Sonkurai by night, we had seen nothing of note. This proved a sore point for a long time, and so I lengthened my statement by reiterating what we had said before, which was that we were escaping to bring to the notice of the outside world the number of deaths occurring daily, and the conditions prevailing along the Thailand/Burma railway, in flagrant violation of the Geneva Convention for prisoners of war.

Apparently, before we had done so, no-one had ever crossed the mountainous jungle country between the Three Pagodas Pass on the borders of Thailand and the coast of Tavoy in Burma, and for a long time we were thought to have been parachuted in to the Burma coast. I have since seen it reported that this area of jungle is second only in density to that in the basin of the Amazon.

After the first two days of questioning our guards became much more vicious, and we were only allowed a ball of rice twice a day, with water to drink. However, it transpired that we were not to be executed after all, and as the work on the railway down to Thailand was not yet sufficiently far forward, it was decided to take us back to Moulmein again.

'*22nd September; Lt. Wakabayashi arrived, with three guards, and we set off north again, travelling by truck. At this last camp, Thanbyuzayat, Capt. Knowles had tried to help by communicating with us, but he was eventually beaten on his face by the Korean guards for so doing.*' We were grateful to him for trying to help us.

'*That night we slept at a railside camp, and the following day we continued our journey, stopping at another camp for a meal, where the Japanese officer there was helpful.*'

To show the conditions prevailing on the railway at this exact time, I quote from the Annual Medical Report, Changi POW Camp, Part 2:

'The task of the medical and administrative staff of 'F' Force was an uphill and losing struggle against malnutrition and disease. The following figures taken from Tanbaya Hospital in mid-September 1943, may give more idea of the magnitude of the struggle. There were in a camp of approximately 1,600 men: 500 beri-beri cases, 521 dysentery cases, 573 malaria cases, and 317 with tropical ulcers. There were never at one time more than six fit medical officers, and fifty trained medical orderlies available to deal with these patients. The rations consisted for all purposes of rice, fresh vegetables and a minute quantity of meat, and the drugs and dressings available were negligible.'

The hospital at Tanbaya was about 60 kilometres north of the Three Pagodas Pass, and it was there that several of our Sappers died, after being evacuated from Sonkurai.

'*We continued our journey to Moulmein, and on arrival were again taken to the Military Police Headquarters. The next day, 24th September, we were once more interrogated by the Kempei-Tai before being taken to Moulmein Gaol, where we spent one night in solitary confinement.*'

'*25th September; Dr. Singh again insisted that we were removed to the hospital wing*', and so we returned to our old ward. There were now cases of cholera in the gaol, and the warders were much more wary of us than they had been before, when we were last there. For the second time Dr. Singh did his utmost for us, and we were allowed to remain for a further ten days.

'*5th October; we were collected by the Moulmein Military Police to make our second journey south, and spent the night at a Police Station, south of Moulmein.*' I am not sure of the village, but our notes here are somewhat indistinct. The name appears to be Tambizyan, but the village was most probably Thanbyuzayat which was, of course, some distance from the railway camp. The Burmese police here were very helpful and fed us well, and the Kempei-Tai returned all our property to us.

'*6th October; we stopped the night at a Burmese military hut, standing on the bank of a large river, where we were allowed to wash.*' This river must have been either the Zami or the Ataran.

The following day: '*7th October; we went on by truck to Sonkurai Camp 2*', the camp from which we had originally escaped, and this we thought the most cruel blow of all. We expected that Lt. Takahashi, who had been in charge of the camp, must have had a bad time at the hands of his superior officers, as we had escaped from under his command, and would, therefore, wish to make things as difficult as possible for us. However, at the beginning of August he had been replaced by Lt. Wakabayashi, of the Malay POW Administration, who treated us fairly.

At other camps, we had never known what would happen to us, but at Sonkurai we were told quite clearly that food would be brought to us twice a day, and that we would be taken down to the river to wash once a day. We lived in a small shelter, made of split bamboos, with enough room for the four of us to lie down at night. This was just outside the main POW camp Area, on the opposite side of the railway track and very near my old cholera isolation camp, of which I still have such terrible memories. I think that by now cholera had taken its toll, and had almost died out. On arrival, all our personal property was taken away from us yet again.

'*It was here at Sonkurai that Lt.-Col. F. J. Dillon was very active on our behalf*', and did all he could to help us in our uncertain position. It was good to be able to see some of our old friends from 'F' Force, as our food was normally brought across from the main camp by a British officer, with whom we were occasionally able to have a quick word or two before the Korean guards rushed up to stop us talking. It was at Sonkurai that we were able to find out a little more of the general war situation.

During the whole period of captivity, a number of extremely brave men risked their lives by operating radio receivers, which had been made from various spare parts, scrounged in the early days at Changi. These 'canaries' were still kept very much underground, and brought out whenever possible to listen to the news. In Changi this had not been so difficult, because eventually there was a mains supply of electricity.

When the various parties left Changi to go up to the railway, the canaries were broken down into small components, and were never discovered in perfunctory inspections. On reaching the railway camps they were reassembled, and converted so that they would work off a 12-volt car or lorry battery. As it was now possible to reach Sonkurai by road, lorries and ambulances would pass occasionally. If one should happen to stop for the night, its battery was borrowed for a short time, enabling us to hear a little more news.

These men who risked their lives to get news of the war did more good for morale than anyone else, and were, to my mind, the bravest of all prisoners. Some were discovered and subsequently beaten to death. Others, whom I came to know later, were cruelly beaten before ending up in Outram Road Gaol in Singapore.

We never stayed anywhere for more than about two days, and sure enough, on the third day, 9th October, the officer bringing our food that morning informed us, rather sheepishly and not very tactfully, that we were being taken to Nieke for execution that afternoon. However, he also said there was a rumour that this might not now take place. Nieke was the Administration Headquarters for this part of the railway, where Col. Banno, the senior Japanese officer, was stationed. We had already met Col. Banno at Thanbyuzayat, where he had interrogated us so forcefully, so we were filled with apprehension.

Shortly afterwards one of our Korean guards rushed up, shouting: 'Speedo! Speedo! All men go to Nieke!' And so, on: '*9th October 1943; we were taken away and put in the back of an army lorry, to be taken to Nieke for execution.*'

These lorries were generally driven by Australians, with a Japanese guard in front with the driver, and a reserve driver in the back with another Japanese guard. Also in the back of the truck with us was Col. Dillon, who had already tried to help us, and now did so again. The guard did not allow him to speak directly to us, but did allow him to talk to the Australian co-driver in the back with us, to whom he said, fairly clearly so that we could all hear: 'I think these four are going to be all right. I don't believe there will be any rough stuff this afternoon'.

This obviously gave us renewed hope, but for how long we had no idea, and I now began to think that execution by firing squad might almost be preferable to our present existence; it would, at least, be a quick death.

'At Nieke we were again put into a similar, but slightly larger shelter, and Col. Banno allowed Capt. Barber, MC, R.A.M.C., to come and see us.' He had, of course, very little in the way of drugs, but he gave me some injections, together with a small amount of morphia that he had. He and Sgt. Innis, R.A.M.C., dressed Moffat's legs and generally did all they possibly could for us. At this time I was having to ask the Japanese guard permission to go to the latrines about every ten minutes. 'Benjo! Benjo! Speedo!' were the words I seemed to be calling all day and all night.

They didn't shoot us, and after a few days it became one of Col. Banno's favourite pastimes just to come and look at us, and then he too allowed us reasonable washing facilities in the river. I think, in a way, we owe our lives to the fact that the Japanese admired us for having beaten the jungle for eight weeks.

The only two other escape attempts, of which I have heard, both ended in execution. One was when two Australian and two British prisoners left Bukit Timah camp and rowed for miles in a small boat, but were executed during the Selarang Incident. The other was when six men attempted an escape from a camp at the southern end of the railway. Four of them were caught soon after escaping and were brought to Chungkai in handcuffs, where they were then shot in a quarry near the camp; the other two were not immediately rearrested, but were soon returned to Tha Makham, where they were made to dig their own graves before being bayonetted to death.

At Nieke we were not badly treated, but we were often interrogated during our four days there. However, there was no further immediate threat of execution.

There is little doubt that we owe our lives to the efforts of all those senior British officers, who had been brought from various railway camps down the line up to Nieke to witness our execution, and in particular to Capt. Cyril Wild, who spoke Japanese with such fluency that he was able to reduce Col. Banno to tears by impressing on him the disgrace and shame that he would bring upon the Emperor and the Imperial Japanese Army if he allowed the execution of what he termed 'these brave men'.

The day of my proposed execution almost coincided with what has become known as 'The Double Tenth', the 10th October 1943, when so many innocent civilian internees and others were rounded up in Singapore for ruthless questioning and, in many cases, sadistic torture by the Kempei-Tai. The Bishop of Singapore was one of these who suffered severely.

'We left Nieke to travel south on 23rd October, stopping at a native wayside camp, where we were ordered to sleep on the ground.'

The two parts of the railway had meantime been joined up on 17th October 1943, near Konkuita, 262.87 kms., with an official Japanese ceremony to be held eight days later on 25th October. The line was now complete from Moulmein to Nong Pladuk, a total distance of 471.30 kms., 415 kms. of which, from Thanbyuzayat to Nong Pladuk, had been completed ahead of schedule in only 12 months, but at an unbelievable cost in human life. I believe that the joining up ceremony was quite an event for the Japanese, with a gun-metal peg being driven into the line at the actual point where the two lines met, and a train, decked with flags, came up to Konkuita. Also, a bronze medallion was cast, bearing the inscription: 'To commemorate the opening to traffic of the railway connecting Thailand with Burma, October, 1943'.

G. P. Adams was working at Konkuita at the time of this celebration, and he tells me:

'Immediately after our return to Konkuita train loads of men would stop in the siding there — some were westbound Jap reinforcements, in good spirits, and excellent health. The eastbound trains were almost too disgusting to describe.

'The first one I saw was filled with Japanese sick and wounded; they had been shut up in those steel 10-ton trucks for many hours, without food or water, and their wounds, all serious, untended since boarding. The POWs were moved to pity and many went forward to offer them water and even a cigarette in some cases. The now useless warriors of the Emperor lay in their own filth, and all were nauseated by the stench of their foul matted bloody dressings. Little wonder that the Japanese High Command were callous to us POWs if they could treat their own kith and kin thus.

'Whatever feelings of horror we had experienced at the sight of the Japanese wounded, it was nothing compared with what awaited us.

'Whilst working POWs of Konkuita had suffered greatly from the slave-drivings of the engineers, both in physical ordeal and the severe mental stresses inherent in Japanese captivity, their condition could not compare with the survivors of the camps between Konkuita and Nikki. Those were the men who had plodded past us in Kinsaiyok back in May and June. Three thousand out of one group of seven thousand had died from every possible disease in less than six months.

'Everyone available rushed forward to help them, and offer them succour, but they were soon on their way back to base and Singapore. It seemed that they had never been properly transferred to the Thailand POW Administration, and been denied proper access to even the meagre food and medical supplies of the original Thailand POWs. It would have taken we cowmen not more than a day, or two, to have driven a few cattle to them, whatever the weather. They told of their experiences as successive trains stopped by us over many days — I heard of the passing of many friends and comrades. The dead could not be removed, for they had to 'attend' roll-call at the base camps!

* * *

'Lt.-General Ishida, Chief of Staff in Thailand, received only 10 years' imprisonment for his responsibility for war crimes concerned with the railway. In his defence he said that he gave instructions that Japanese soldiers should treat prisoners working on the Burma–Siam railway as 'brothers and children of God', that he urged unit commanders to improve camp conditions, and reported to the Japanese C-in-C that there were medical facilities available for less than one third of the total number sick.

'Korean guard E. Hayashi, known as 'The Maggot', was hanged at Changi in 1947, after an Australian War Crimes Court had sentenced him to death for having kicked in the stomach a sick Australian POW who did not stand to attention quickly enough when Hayashi entered a hut at Nikki in Siam on the 'death railway' – the Australian died soon afterwards.

* * *

'F' and 'H' Forces

'These forces, together with the small 'L' force, believed to comprise nine doctors and sixty orderlies, should be the subject of their own book . . . I was fortunate not to have shared their terrible experiences, when I was living so close to their own camps.'

(iii) Back to Singapore

At the same time that the railway line was built, the rough track alongside it was worked on and improved, by POWs, for the use of Jap transport. It was along this track that we were driven, although I cannot remember clearly, but we might have travelled some of the way down by train, as I can recall being in one of the railway trucks normally used for carrying rails. It is hard to be completely accurate about our mode of transport, as we were so ill at the time.

In this way we continued our southward journey, stopping at various camps down the line to be exhibited to the POWs as a deterrent to anyone with escape in mind. At several camps the prisoners had been made to build pyres for our cremation, but this was also for deterrent purposes.

'*Eventually, we reached Kanburi on 24th October*', cross-ing the new steel bridge that had now been completed at Tha Makham. The first night we slept in the Japanese guard room, but the next day we were put in a deep pit near the guard house, and I believe this pit was often used for purposes such as this. We were allowed a visit from a British medical officer, and were fed by the British POWs, who cheered us greatly by walking past, discussing loudly topics which they thought might be of interest to us, including any war news.

'*25th October; we left Kanburi by truck for Ban Pong*', and thus we had completed on foot one way, and by truck and train the other way, the double length of the Thailand section of the railway.

'*At midnight we entrained in a rice truck, and arrived at Padang Besar in the early morning of 27th October. Here we remained in the station until evening, when we left for Singapore, travelling third class. We spent three days in the train and were fed from the restaurant car.*' In our compart-ment were Japanese soldiers and about 15 to 20 young girls; we didn't know who these girls were, but we referred to them as the 'Japanese Comfort Corps'. They were not in uniform, and appeared to be camp followers, perhaps making the lives of their troops a little brighter. They were certainly kind to us, giving us extra little luxuries to eat with our rather dull fare, including small bread rolls, which were the first we had tasted since our arrival in Singapore nearly two years ago.

We certainly travelled south to Singapore in more comfort than on our original journey north in rice trucks and, although crowded, at least we had seats and were able to see the country. To me this looked especially beautiful, as I was seeing for the first time for so long wide open views over cultivated land and paddy fields, with small kampongs dotted here and there, each framed with its own palm trees. We also travelled through rubber plantations, where the Tamils were busy tapping the latex, and paying little attention to the passing train.

There were occasional halts to pick up fuel, water and rations, but as we were a troop train no-one was allowed to get down, even when we stopped in the main stations, such as Kuala Lumpur. However, the Japanese girls bought sweets and peanut-brittle from vendors who came to the windows, and generously gave some to us. Our guards never prevented this; they all seemed happy at the thought of going to Singapore, because they too must have been living under harsh conditions. On the journey we shared their food, which was little better than that we had received in the POW camps.

And so finally, on: '*30th October 1943; we arrived back in Singapore*', but still with no idea what the future might hold for us.

(iv) Outram Road Gaol

After leaving Singapore Station, we were taken by truck to what I think was a police post in Robinson Road, where our finger prints were taken and we were made to sit, holding a numbered placard while they photographed us; just like the normal pictures of criminals or wanted persons.

Our next visit was to Raffles College for further interrogation. This questioning, each time by different people, seemed endless, and in fact our answers to previous sessions were always in the possession of the current investigator. I cannot imagine why they were still trying to trap us into saying something which did not entirely agree with our earlier verbal or written statements, as they had all the evidence they required if we should be brought to trial.

One investigator quoted from one of my previous written statements made in Burma, that I had seen very little of Japanese activities in Malaya and Thailand, as we had travelled either by closed trucks, or by night. He now said that this no longer applied, as we had travelled the whole length of the railway, from Moulmein to Singapore, without visual restriction. I had to agree with this, but pointed out to him that I was no longer in a position to attempt an escape, in order to pass on any information that I might have gathered. And so it always went on.

We were then driven to Outram Road Gaol, of whose evil reputation we had heard when in Changi. This gaol was

administered by the Kempei-Tai, and it was here that most of
the barbaric tortures took place. Prior to the war it had been
the Civilian Gaol for Singapore, but it was now the Punishment Gaol for the whole of South-East Asia, and housed
Chinese, Malays, and many of their own Imperial Japanese
troops who had transgressed their laws in some way. These
men certainly received no better treatment than we did.

On arrival in the gaol, we were stripped naked and given
the most thorough search possible. Again we were questioned
about our activities, and a written inventory was taken of our
few possessions. Proceedings were held up while the prison
guards looked at photographs of our children, and in the
meantime we were still standing naked, explaining who
they were.

We were each given prison clothing, comprising a loose
jacket and a pair of trousers, and were then taken to our
respective solitary cells. Mine was D41 (D Shi-Ju-Ichi), and
my prison number, to which I had to answer so many hundreds of times at *tenko*, was 557 (Go-Hyaku-Go-Ju-Nana).

Our cells must have measured about ten feet by four feet.
They each had a concrete floor and a solid wooden door at
one end, in which was a small inspection grille and a trap-
door, through which a dish of food could be pushed from the
outside. On the wall, opposite the door, a small barred
window stood about eight feet up from the ground, and a
plain electric light bulb hung from the ceiling. This bright
light was left on day and night.

The furnishings comprised three wooden planks on the
floor, which formed my bed, and one wooden shaped neck
block, 18 inches long by 6 inches square, with the edges
rounded off, which was my pillow. I also had two blankets,
and a latrine bucket in the corner by the door. This bucket
was emptied only once a day, by a 'trustie', trusties being the
prisoners who were allowed out of their cells for fatigues of
this sort.

During the day we were not allowed to lie down, so spent
most of our time sitting on the floor, leaning against the wall.
We all tried to keep our circulations going by doing rather
mild exercises, being too weak to do anything too strenuous,

but this was frowned on by our guards, who moved quietly up and down the cell passage in their 'sneakers', peering through the grille into the cells every now and then.

Periodically we were taken out in small groups to wash, but this was by no means every day. Occasionally at these times the guard, armed with a three-inch paint-brush and a bucket of iodine, slapped this agonizing stuff on our penis' and testicles, with the object, presumably, of preventing or curing scrotal dermatitis, from which most of us suffered, and ringworm, which was very prevalent; indeed, my beard was full of it.

Food was pretty sparse, normally being a bowl of rice and a little warm fish-head soup. I knew it was fish-head, because if we were lucky, we got an eye in the soup; these were too tough to eat, but provided something to suck for a bit. We were not allowed spoons, as the Japanese thought we might try to damage ourselves with them, and so we had to use chopsticks.

We had absolutely nothing in the way of books or paper. However, I managed to record the number of days I was there, 52 in all from 30th October to 21st December 1943, by making marks on the whitewashed walls of the cell with a fishbone, which I kept hidden under my bed planks. I had one friend who visited me at night, and this was a small mouse, for whom I kept back a grain or two of rice each day.

By this time my beri-beri, from which I had suffered for a long time, became much worse. This is a disease caused by lack of Vitamin B, in which one's whole body becomes full of fluid. If I pressed my finger into my leg, it took a long time for the indentation to disappear, and from being almost a skeleton, I was now full of fluid and swollen all over. Then, suddenly, I passed water almost incessantly for a few days, and returned to my emaciated condition, but very much weaker.

Sometimes I fainted when trying to get to the trap-door for my food. Another prisoner, an Australian officer, Lt. P. V. Dean, 2/4 M.G. Battalion, A.I.F., had been given the job of distributing the food and, if he saw me unconscious on the floor, he called the guard to open the cell, in order to try and bring me round. I owe a lot to him for my survival, as I think

many others do, too. It was he who told me that, with any
luck, I might be sent back to Changi, owing to the state of
my health and the bother I was causing the IJA by having to
unlock my cell so often.

I don't know why Dean was in Outram Road, but he had
been in for a long time before I arrived, and had become the
leader of the small group of trusties who distributed the food
and emptied our latrine buckets. He was a strong, cheerful
character, and I always felt that he exerted a certain influ-
ence over the junior Japanese guards. If he called for them to
bring the Sergeant-in-Charge ('The Cat'), he generally came.

Mr. S. Gunaratnam, a civilian prisoner and Dean's number
two in the group of trusties, was also extremely helpful and,
in fact, he wrote to me after the war; I quote his letter later
in this chapter.

When Dean mentioned to me that I might be sent back to
Changi because of my health, I conceived the idea of putting
in a few extra faints of my own. I would lie, face downwards
on the concrete floor, but on one occasion I was nearly
caught out when 'The Cat' came in and tickled the undersides
of my feet with a feather. Luckily, I had lost most of my reflexes and my sense of feeling, so did not give myself away.
(Incidentally, I have no feeling in the soles of my feet today.)

To try and get back to Changi I even tried breaking my
arm. To do this, I put my wrist on the floor and my upper
arm on the 'pillow', and beat my arm with one of the wooden
bed planks; but when one is so weak, it is difficult to wield
a plank with enough force to break an arm. Perhaps I simply
had not the guts to do it hard enough but, in any event, the
attempt was unsuccessful, and all I got was a very sore arm.

For the last six weeks of my time in Outram Road I was
unable to get up or move at all, and I was determined, at all
costs, that I would somehow get out of this gaol. I had
known of its reputation before I came; few came out alive,
and many went mad. Some prisoners would shout all night,
and for two nights we heard repeated crashes, as if someone
was charging against a door. After this had ceased, one of
the trusties told me that a prisoner had killed himself by
banging his head against the door during the night. The

Japs had a great fear of madness.

As we had no material for writing, and no books to read, I tried to preserve my sanity by working out quite complicated mathematical problems in my head. I now decided, definitely, that if ever I got home I would take up farming; at times like this one feels the need to be near the earth. I am not a particularly religious man, but in that solitary cell I prayed.

This is the letter I received from Gunaratnam, after the war:

> S. Gunaratnam,
> c/o No. 13, Leong Sin Nam St.,
> Ipoh,
> Malayan Union.
>
> 14th May 1946

Dear Lieut. Bradley,

I am sure you will be greatly surprised to hear from me. This is your friend '606' of cell D42 calling you from good old Malaya.

This letter will take you back to those bad old days in 1943 when we were together in the Big House, with you in cell D41. You were having a rotten time then. Do you remember how often Lieut. Dean and myself had to go to your cell when you fell unconscious to bring you round? Do you still remember the Old Cat who approved the milk diet for you, and the Witch Doctor who always grumbled at me for calling him to give you camphor and vitamin injections? Remember how Lieut. Dean would call you a bad boy when we woke you?

I should say you were one of the luckiest of the lot at the Outram Road Gaol, for no one who came in your condition ever returned home. You were really a brave one for having taken things so smilingly.

I was very glad to hear that you were getting better at Changi Camp. I was sorry to have missed you after the Japanese surrender. I wrote to the RAPWI and obtained your address.

I have already written to many of my friends abroad who sent me testimonials and gifts. I hope you will be kind enough to write a few words, mentioning my assistance rendered in the Gaol. I am sure they will prove a great help to me here.

At present I am unemployed, and prospect of getting something to do soon is very dark. I am having a tough time trying to make both ends meet. Cost of living here is still high, and money just evaporates from one's pockets. But when it comes to trying to get some money, well, it's just another task of Hercules.

How are you getting on now? Fit and kicking? And how are things over there? I am pretty certain your place must be quite a paradise — at least it is, when compared to our Malaya.

Well, good-bye and the best of luck.

I am hoping to hear from you soon.

> Yours sincerely,
> (Signed) S. G. ATNAM
> (Late '606' of Cell D42, Big House)

P.S. If you happen to meet Capt. Anchor, please give him my best wishes. Is it possible to let me have his address? Thanks.

(v) Back to Changi

On 21st December 1943, after about eight weeks in solitary confinement, I was finally evacuated back to Changi Hospital, which had now been transferred from Roberts Barracks to Selarang Barracks, and the Japanese were again meticulous about handing back my few personal belongings. Bill Anker was evacuated at the same time, and later on Ian Moffat and finally Guy Machado were also brought out of Outram Road. However, it was 9th March 1944 before Machado eventually joined us, and he had been in Outram Road for four and a half months.

I was put into a proper iron bed, and would have been reasonably comfortable had I not been so ill. Indeed, I almost had to learn to walk again. Col. Julian Taylor, Consulting Surgeon Malaya Command, came to see me, and was particularly interested in the fact that I had no nails on my fingers or toes. He will always be remembered with great affection by ex POWs for the wonderful work he did, as a prisoner, in the Changi Hospital. He used to come and talk to me about sailing, as we found this was a mutual interest of ours, and I believe he kept his boat in Chichester Harbour, from where I was later to do much of my sailing.

My tremendous beard was exceedingly ugly, being partly eaten away by ringworm, but thankfully, I was now able to have this shaved off. Major E. J. Harper, who commanded 560 Field Company, R.E., and who knew me well, came to see me, but not recognizing me at all, had to ask one of the orderlies where I was.

It was while I was in hospital here that I received my third letter from Lindsay, enclosing a lovely photograph of Roger, now aged five, with a friend, Penny Knowles. This was a wonderful thing to have, and it must have arrived during my time in Outram Road and been held for me in Changi.

During captivity people normally trust one another and try to help each other. However, during my time in bed I was let down badly by the two Australian drivers who had driven us to our intended execution at Nieke, and who had now returned south. They had been driving for the Japanese for some considerable time, and were still making trips down into Singapore with them.

They came to see me in my ward and asked whether they could do anything to help, as they had the opportunity to get hold of almost anything when in Singapore. I told them that I now had no money, except some travellers cheques, but this, they said, was no problem. I handed over my cheques for them to cash, and they promised to bring me eggs, biscuits, and if possible a chicken. That was the last I saw of those two Aussies, but I suppose it was my fault for being so naïve.

I learnt later that these two were pretty unscrupulous, and had managed to get money from other suckers like myself. But they were the great exception to the rule, as Australians as a whole, I believe, stood up to the rigours of captivity better than the rest of the Allies. They were more conscious of the necessity of really good hygiene, and they were certainly very much more enterprising than the rest of us. They were also great opportunists, but nearly always shared with others the gains of their successful deals.

I now had no money, but had learnt my lesson. Above all I had achieved my aim of coming out of Outram Road alive, and only prayed that I would never have to return there. Nothing could change my determination to get home to my family. This resolve had kept me going so far, and I was certain that I should now be able to overcome my present state of health and survive, although I was mystified by the fact that I had not been brought before a Court Martial.

Bill and I were allowed to remain in Selarang Hospital for about three and a half months, and it was towards the end of this time that Machado and Moffat joined us from Outram Road. We were permanent bed patients, but were gradually getting stronger again. The Japanese had told us that we had lost all rank as officers, through our escape attempt, and we were not, in fact, in an officers' ward, but this worried us not at all.

From the end of March 1944 onwards, the existence of the hospital at Selarang was complicated by the practice of the IJA authorities of edging the camp away from the aerodrome, which was being built by the POW labour force that had not gone up country.

On 25th April 1944 orders were received for the regrouping and concentration of all POWs at Changi Gaol, with the exception of the hospital, the greater part of which would move to Woodlands, Kranji, on the northern part of the Island within a very short distance of the causeway joining Singapore to the mainland, and the lesser part to Changi Gaol. The main part of the hospital moved by lorry to Kranji, and after some discussion the medical authorities decided to risk taking us with them; the problem being that we were really still in the hands of the Kempei-Tai, who had, in fact, already made one visit to Selarang to inspect us.

However, the move went smoothly, and was completed by 25th May 1944, and the remainder moved to huts outside the perimeter wall of Changi Gaol by the end of the month.

Kranji was predominantly British, while Changi Hospital was mostly Australian.

This was a time of great change as Changi Gaol, built to house 600, had been occupied by 3,500 men, women and children internees since the fall of Singapore, and these poor wretched people were now moved to camps in Singapore so that 12,000 POWs could move in. However, over half of these had to live in makeshift huts and shelters outside the main perimeter wall of the gaol.

At Kranji we were housed in wooden huts, but now in an officers' ward, and we settled down to a new, more comfortable life of waiting, but all the time I had a sneaking worry of uncertainty. Had the Japanese really lost interest in us, and were we to be left here until the end of the war? What would our fate be when the end came? Would they massacre us all?

We had not been forgotten, for a guard arrived after about two days and took us to Changi Gaol, where two small wards had been opened for those inmates of Outram Road Gaol, whose health even the Japanese felt unprepared to accept. These wards had originally been part of the Gaol Hospital in peacetime; one was on the ground floor, which housed other ranks, and the upper one was for officers.

Here we met John Wyett, from Hobart, Tasmania, who was in Intelligence, 8th Australian Infantry Division. He became a very great friend of ours, and has since visited both Bill and me after the war, but strangely enough none of us knew why he had been put in Outram Road. Through him we were to meet many friends.

Jack Macalister was in the R.A.A.F., and had been shot down over Timor. He had made two efforts to seize Japanese planes in an attempt to escape; with locals he had started diversionary fires, but on each occasion the plane he had chosen was not airworthy; one had a flat battery, and I forget what was wrong with the other. I think his problems would have been great, even had he been able to get away, flying a plane with Japanese markings.

Roberts, another Australian, was in some way connected with the Red Cross, but he was a silent man and none of us really got to know him.

Shortly after our move to Changi Gaol there arrived four officers who had been discovered operating an illicit radio at Kanburi, on the railway. These four were Major W. G. Smith who, before the war, had been in the Public Works Department in Singapore, was fifty years old at the time and is still alive today, a very old man; Major Jim Slater, R.A., from Yorkshire who, sadly, died not long after the war at a fairly young age; Morton Mackay, a Canadian from British Columbia, who died recently; and Eric Lomax from Scotland. Eric had been shock-ingly beaten up before being brought down to Outram Road— both his arms were completely misshapen, having been broken and never reset—but I am glad to say he survived and is alive and well.

The story of these men should be the subject of a book on its own. There were nine of them altogether who were arrested in Kanburi in September 1943. Two, Capt. Jack Hawley, R.A.S.C. and Lt. Armitage, R.A., were beaten to death. The others were court-martialled in Bangkok before being brought to Outram Road on 30th November 1943. Besides Smith, Slater, Mackay and Lomax there was Sgt. Fred Smith, R.A., who only got out of Outram Road at the end of the war in 1945, C. L. A. Thew, who did not accompany his companions to Outram Road but was brought there on 26th February 1945, and Major Harry Knight, F.M.S.V.F., an Australian, who died in Changi having been brought out of Outram Road. The Japanese brought prisoners out only when they were on the point of death. It was bad for statistics for too many to die in Outram Road. These were the men who risked everything so that the rest of the prisoners might know something of the world outside. They were indeed brave men.

On 12th June 1944 Machado, who had been taken back to Outram Road for further interrogation, was again released and returned to Changi, and his weight on arrival was 105 lbs.

There was also in our ward a charming Dutch naval officer, Waudenburg, who had been captured in Sumatra, but sadly they took him away, and later we were told that he had been executed. The date of his trial was 26th November 1944 and he was executed on 31st January 1945. The charges against him were espionage, breach of Military Security Act, preparation for helping enemy to attack.

We were now allowed to receive daily visits from a medical officer, and the one who looked after us was Major E. A. Rogers, R.A.A.M.C., ('Bon' to everyone). Before the war Bon was known as the best dressed man in Tasmania, and also as the 'Ladies Doctor'. Of course, he had practically no drugs with which to treat us, but he was, without doubt, the most cheerful man in adversity that I have ever met, and we always looked forward to his visits. He made us feel better each time he entered our ward.

In the ward below us there was a real north-countryman from the Manchester Regiment, called Strange. He attached himself to me as unofficial batman, and after the war he came down to work on my farm in Sussex. He was a mole catcher by trade, and his wife had one of the best coats in the district, made from the skins of all the many moles he had caught! However, after two or three years he returned to his native Glossop, as he said he could understand Japanese better than the southern accent of Sussex!

We remained in this ward in Changi Gaol for one month, all the time wondering if and when we would be taken for trial for the 'crime' we had committed in escaping from Sonkurai. We had been moved around so much recently, and all we wanted was to stay where we were, but felt sure we should not be allowed to do so. Eventually, on 26th June 1944, Japanese guards arrived to take us away, and we said goodbye to the friends we had made in the ward, hoping so much that we would be returned to them again, but at the same time being extremely apprehensive that we might be taken back to Outram Road. We all felt that we were fortunate in having survived our deprivations in this fearful gaol, and the thought of being there again was our main dread.

I was to learn later that, just before I was put in Outram Road Gaol, one of the most heroic and incredible missions took place, but it remained completely unknown to prisoners-of-war until after the cessation of hostilities. This operation was code-named 'Jaywick'.

Fourteen men, under the command of Major Ivan Lyon of

Gordon Highlanders, sailed from Australia in an ex-Japanese fishing boat, *Krait*, to within about fifteen miles of Singapore Harbour. This body of men, known as 'Z' Force, after transferring into two-man skin-covered canoes, entered the harbour under cover of darkness on 26th September 1943. They placed limpet mines with time fuses on most of the large ships before rejoining the *Krait*, which they successfully sailed back to Australia. Seven ships, totalling 40,000 tons, were destroyed that night, and the Japanese in no way knew how and by whom the operation had been accomplished.

The following year, 1944, Ivan Lyon, by now promoted to Lieutenant-Colonel, formed a larger party of twenty-three men, including those original heroes from 'Z' Force, with the intention of making a further raid on Japanese shipping in Singapore Harbour. This expedition was to be code-named 'Operation Rimau' (Tiger). This force sailed from Garden Island, Western Australia, in a British submarine, H.M.S. *Porpoise*, and after transferring to a large Malay junk they headed for Singapore. They hoped to repeat their previous successful operation, entering the harbour in small semi-submersible boats. Unfortunately, they were spotted by the Japanese and thirteen of the party, including Lt.-Col. Lyon, were killed. The remaining ten were eventually taken prisoner and brought to Outram Road Gaol, but the Japanese never found any evidence to connect this raid with the earlier 'Jaywick'.

Almost nothing would have been known about what followed but for the fact that Eric Lomax had been taken back from Changi to Outram Road Gaol to finish his sentence of five years. He had the unenviable job of emptying the latrine buckets from the cells, but at least he was able to communicate with the inmates of those cells. He was, therefore, probably the only person to know the ten apprehended men of 'Operation Rimau'.

A formal Court-Martial took place on 5th July 1945, under the presidency of Colonel Towatori. The charge was Breach of Martial Law (Stratagem (or Perfidy) and Espionage). One of the chief accusations was that they did not wear badges of rank and hence were in breach of International Law because they were not wearing recognised military uniforms. Inevitably, the entire party were sentenced to death but, what was surprising and probably without precedent, was that at the conclusion of the trial Colonel Towatori shook hands with each man and addressed the group collectively as 'heroes'. On 7th July 1945 the ten 'Rimau' men were taken from Outram Road Gaol to a place in the open country, near Bukit Timah, where they were beheaded by five warrant officer prison guards from Outram Road. Thus there were no survivors of 'Operation Rimau'.

At the end of the war the ten bodies were exhumed from three graves where they had been thrown in, one on top of the other. Five were blindfolded and the other five were not. It appeared that each executioner had one blindfold which he used for both of his victims. From the extensive research on this subject done by Harold Lander of New South Wales I have learnt that the executioners were reported to have laughed, joked and boasted of their prowess when they got back to the warders' room in Outram Road. In Singapore at that time the Japanese tended to hand out the job of executing prisoners as a favour and to keep up morale.

One of the five 'executioners' committed suicide after the war. The other four were charged with Outram Road atrocities and received prison terms ranging from five to ten years. The convict warder who was in charge of the gravediggers was also up on atrocity charges and he got seven years.

A point of interest to me is the fact that the chief prosecutor at the trial of these 'Rimau' men, Major Haruo Kamiya, was one of the three judges officiating at my trial. Furuta was the interpreter at both trials, as indeed he was at the trial of Lomax and his party in Bangkok.

(vi) Trial

We were not forgotten as, on 26th June 1944, almost ten months after our recapture, Japanese guards arrived and took us away by lorry. We had no idea where we were going, but for the first time our few sad possessions were not collected up and confiscated. Did this mean that we should no longer need them, or did it mean we should be returning after perhaps more questioning?

We drove down to Singapore, not to Outram Road, but to a building which Machado knew and identified as Raffles College. Here we were told, by the interpreter, that we were going to be tried by Court Martial, and we were ushered into a room that had been prepared for this purpose.

There was a high stage at one end of the room, on which sat all the Japanese officials behind their desks, while we sat on chairs in the main part of the room. However, we had to stand, of course, during questioning and when our sentences were pronounced.

The Presiding Judge was Major Yoshiraru Omomo, who had with him Judge Major Haruo Kamiya, the Judicial Officer, and Judge Captain Mokusaburo Nakamura. The Prosecuting Officer was Lt. H. Hori; we had no Defending Officer, and there was no British officer present. There was a Japanese interpreter, whose name was later confirmed to be Furuta. He was, apparently, called as a witness during the subsequent investigations into War Crimes.

During the proceedings we were all cross-examined, one by one. As before, we were asked the reason for our escape, and what information we had proposed to give to the British authorities, had our escape proved successful. As on all previous occasions, we stuck to our original statement, which was that our one and only reason for escaping was to bring to the notice of the outside world the conditions prevailing in the camps along the Thailand/Burma railway.

The charges against us were read out in Court, but it was difficult to understand them, as Furuta, the interpreter, was not easy to follow, and it was only after the war, when I was given a copy of the summary of the trial, that I fully understood the nature of these charges. It seemed, at the time, that I was actually being accused of keeping within me cholera germs, an extraordinary charge.

The whole trial was conducted in Japanese, through the interpreter, and our investigators kept on insisting that we had been homesick as a result of the conditions under which we worked, and so had deserted our men. The Prosecutor never used the word 'escape', but always referred to it as 'decamping' or 'running away', but this could have been a loose interpretation by Furuta. As there was no Defending Officer, there was nothing we could do but strongly attack their whole attitude towards POWs working on the railway.

The trial took place in a reasonably ordered manner, and no force whatsoever was used to try to extract answers from us. In fact, we were given very little opportunity to express any views that we held until the end of the trial, and then we were only allowed to answer direct questions. Whether Furuta was giving a fair translation of our answers, we had no means of knowing, but in any event the charges brought against us show that our motives for escaping were totally misconstrued, and that the Japanese were determined to portray us as deserters. However, during the War Crimes Trials after the war, Furuta did endorse our statements, saying that we had attacked the conditions under which men were being forced to work.

The whole Court Martial was a mere formality. The Judges had already decided on the sentences beforehand, and did not even appear to communicate with one another before announcing their findings, and delivering sentence. Bill Anker, as the senior officer, was given nine years' hard labour, and the other three of us eight years. This meant solitary confinement.

At the end of the proceedings, the Presiding Judge came down into the body of the Courtroom, and made us walk round in a circle in front of him. We realized he was making up his mind as to whether or not we were fit enough to go back to Outram Road to serve our sentences and, with this in mind, we stumbled round, trying to look as if we were at death's door. Of course, we had not seen the sun, or been in the fresh air, for almost a year, so we must have looked pretty ghastly; nor were we the best dressed of defendants, while the Japanese were immaculate in their dress.

Thankfully, he decided not to return us to Outram Road, but to our hospital ward inside the walls of Changi Gaol. He told us, as we had already been informed earlier, that we had lost all rank as officers, and that we were to be allowed no contact at all with other officers. We learnt later that officers now lived in the huts outside the prison wall, as work on the aerodrome had been going on for some time, and accommodation space was becoming very limited. This is where, I believe, the collective noun, 'A Quarrel of Colonels', originated. In this ward we would be subject to intermittent Japanese medical inspections, to ascertain whether we were fit enough to go back to solitary confinement.

Having decided thus, the Presiding Judge acted in a characteristically unpredictable manner by giving us each a small bag of sweets, and telling us to take 'the greatest care' of our health! This bears out my feeling that the findings of the court were a foregone conclusion, otherwise it is unlikely that the Presiding Judge would have had four bags of sweets in court with him, ready to give to us.

I have always felt that the Japanese were very susceptible to their environment. Immediately after hostilities, when we were at Changi camp on Singapore Island in more or less civilized surroundings, they behaved towards us in a civilized manner. At the jungle camps along the railway they appeared to lose this veneer of civilization, and almost revert to the laws of the jungle, where they became totally unpredictable and ruthless, although of course there were always exceptions to the rule. The Allies, in some cases, were by no means perfect.

Col. C. H. D. Wild found this summary of our trial after the war, during the War Crimes Investigations in Singapore, and this I now quote, together with a covering letter, both of which he sent back to England:

'Walter Henry Angker   Prisoner of War (British
                              Captain) 35 years of age
                              The 4th Branch of Malay
                              POW Camp.

James Bottomley Bradley   Prisoner of War (British
                              Lieutenant) 33 years old

Ian Marson Moffat   Prisoner of War (British
                              Lieutenant) 27 years old

Guy Alfred Marchyard   Prisoner of War (British 2nd
                              Lieutenant) 37 years old

The case of violence of Prisoner of War Act by the above accused persons has been tried in this Court Martial, with Lt. H. Hori, a judicial officer as the inspecting prosecutor, and verdicted the case as follows:

TEXT
The accused person Angker, is sentenced to nine years of penal servitude.

The accused persons, Bradley, Moffat and Marchyard are sentenced to eight years each of penal servitude.

REASON
The accused persons Angker, Bradley, Moffat and Marchyard belonged to the British Army and were participated in the fightings in Malaya and became prisoners of war on 15th Feb. 1942 on the Singapore Island. They were received, since the end of May of the same year, at the 2nd Detachment of the 4th Branch of Malay POW Camp, and were engaged in the construction of Siam–Burmese Railways which was carried out by the Oka 5815 Butai (Unit).

The First: The accused Angker was fairly fed up with the extended POW life and was under nostalgic mood, when, on 1st July, 1943, was confided by Mikel Thomas Wilkinson (a British Lieutenant-Colonel, died on 5th August in the course of his flight) of his plan of decamping and was asked to join the decamping party. The accused acceeded to this request and together with seven other decamping party, headed by Lieut. Col. Wilkinson, ran away from the camp early in the morning of 5th July and while on the way to India was apprehended by the Japanese Garrison at the Arkhan Village, Moulmein, Burma on 21st August of the same year.

The Second: The accused, Bradley, was isolated at that time at the detached place in Sonkurai under suspicion of keeping in him cholera germs and the fear for cholera drove him to bitter home-sick, when he was urged by above-mentioned Wilkinson, at the end of June, 1943, to join his decamping party. Acceeding to this request, he ran away from the camp together with other members of the party and was apprehended by the Japanese Garrison in the same manner as Angker.

The Third: The accused person, Moffat, was, from fear of cholera which was furiously raging in Sonkurai at that time, longing for returning home and was detesting the POW life and so when he was asked on 4th July by the afore-mentioned Wilkinson to join the run-away party, he gladly accepted it and joining the party, deserted the camp with other members but was captured at the same place and in the same manner as other members.

The Fourth: The accused Marchyard was working as ration supplier to the cholera patients but actually seeing every day the terribly disasterous scene where patients of cholera die one after another in a limitless number, he was horrified with it and his nostalgic mood drove him to a complete detestation of POW life. In such a time, Captain Jones, a POW died on 17th August in 1943 on his way of flight, confided him on 3rd July 1943 the plan of decamping headed by Lieut. Col. Wilkinson and asked his participation in it. He approved of this, made a run away and was apprehended in the same manner as other members of the party.

The above facts are recognized with the following evidences:
1. Statements of each accused person at this court.
2. Report made by Sergeant Kyuhei Yoshizawa, chief of the 2nd Detachment, the 4th Branch of Malay POW camp.
3. Report made by Deputy Chief of Moulmein Military Police Detachment concerning apprehension and investigation of decamped prisoners of war.
4. Affidavit of Alan Tribilian Hingston, a Lieutenant-Colonel, POW Commandant of the 2nd Detachment, 4th Branch of Malay POW Camp.

5. Lieut.-Col. Wilkinson's will kept at this court.

The deed of each accused person falls under the latter paragraph of the POW Act and so we preferred the "penal servitude for a term" to this case and verdicted as per the Text.

	26th day of June, 1944
	The Summary Court Martial
	of the 7th Area Army.
Presiding Judge:	Major Yoshiharu Omomo
Judge:	Major (Judicial Officer) Haruo Kamiya
Judge:	Captain Mokusaburo Nakamura

The execution of penal servitude was suspended on 19th August, 1945.'

Covering note by Col. C. H. D. Wild:
'*Trial of ANKER, BRADLEY, MOFFAT and MACHADO*
These four officers escaped from "F" Force in Thailand in July 1943. I was warned by Col. Banno's Headquarters to hold myself in readiness to go to Sonkurai Camp and see them shot on their recapture. With permission of Lt.-Col. S. W. Harris, OBE, R.A., Senior British Officer of "F" Force, I saw Col. Banno, who said that these officers had deserted their men in trouble. I replied that, on the contrary, the Japanese having made it impossible for them to look after their men, and being themselves unwilling to see them die by hundreds, they had been prepared to risk their own lives in an attempt to escape to India and let the British army and the outside world know how the Japanese treated their prisoners on the Thailand railway. I also told Col. Banno that when we left Singapore we were told to trust in the Imperial Japanese Army and no harm would come to us. Three months later 1,700 of those who had trusted in the

Imperial Japanese Army were dead and hundreds more were dying. At this Lt.-Col. Banno rather surprisingly started to weep.

To do him justice, it appears that he did prevent these four from being executed, and although they were given 9/10 years imprisonment they were all brought out from Outram Prison on grounds of ill health after two or three months and did not serve the rest of their sentences.

When these four officers were imprisoned at Sonkurai Camp on recapture before being sent to Singapore for court-martial, I managed to tell them that their only line of defence must be that which I had taken with Banno. As expected, the Japanese tried to impute motives of cowardice and self-interest to them, but all four stuck to this line of defence, coupled with a strenuous attack in court on the conditions on the Thailand railway. (This was confirmed recently by Furuta, the Interpreter.) In spite of this the Jap court-martial summary shows that they were sentenced on trumped up charges which put their motives for escape in a very poor light.'

I would like to end this chapter with a tribute to Col. Cyril Wild, because it is to him that I feel I owe so much. There is no doubt in my mind that he saved my life, and it is such a tragedy that he lost his own in an air crash at Kai Tak, Hong Kong in 1946, after having done so much for his fellow men in the war.

Cyril Wild's name will probably always be associated with the surrender at Singapore in February 1942 when, to his great sorrow, he carried the white flag of truce to Japanese headquarters, and also when he acted as interpreter for Lord Louis Mountbatten, who accepted the Japanese surrender in 1945. He was made a Full Colonel during the War Crimes Investigations.

There is very little that one can add to his obituary, written by Lt.-Gen. A. E. Percival, after his untimely death at the age of 38:

COLONEL C. H. D. WILD

Lieutenant-General A. E. Percival writes:

'I write on behalf of all who served in Malaya in 1941–42 and who afterwards experienced the rigours of three and a half years of captivity in Japanese hands, to express our heartfelt sorrow at the tragic death of Cyril Wild in an air accident at Hong Kong on September 25th, 1946.

Before the war Wild was in business in Japan, where, in addition to becoming a fluent Japanese speaker, he acquired a wide knowledge of the characteristics and mentality of the Japanese. In 1941 he became a valuable member of the General Staff of the 3rd Indian Corps in Malaya. His sound judgment, ability, and enthusiasm marked him out as an officer of great promise. It was, however, during the period of captivity that he found the greatest scope for his talents. As interpreter he fought for the interests of his fellow prisoners with unflinching and never failing courage. There were few, either on Singapore Island or in those camps in Siam where he was stationed, who did not at some time or other benefit directly or indirectly from his efforts. After the war he continued his work by accepting an appointment as War Crimes Liaison Officer under the South-East Asia Command, in which capacity he was still serving at the time of his death.'

Cyril Wild was known, by the Japanese, as 'the tall man who never slept'. I think this illustrates his unceasing efforts for others.

EPILOGUE

Chapter 8

EPILOGUE

(i) Last Days of Captivity

IT FELT WONDERFUL to be back again in our ward inside Changi Gaol, but of course it was not easy to live with the permanent fear that the Japanese might appear, at any time, and decide that we were fit to go back to Outram Road, as we were some of the very few who had come out alive.

It was now, when the four of us were together, that we decided to put down some notes about our escape and subsequent recapture. Machado made the first entries, leaving spaces between each so that we could all add any relevant information. I know that in my entries I used no names, but only initials, so that should the notes fall into Jap hands, they would be less able to identify anyone who had shown kindness or had given help to us. Some of the handwriting was not good, and it has taken much time to decipher the notes, even with a magnifying glass.

The Japanese M.O.'s made several surprise visits, and in fact took back Moffat and Macalister, but fortunately released them again later. Bon Rogers, our doctor, was a master at dealing with these Japanese medicals. He would bring them to one of our beds, telling them how he would treat this particular case at home, and then he would ask the Japanese for his opinion. Before waiting for his answer, which of course had to be explained through an interpreter, Bon had moved on to another 'desperately ill' patient, where this tactic would be repeated, thus giving the Japanese little time to consider whether or not we had recovered sufficiently to return to Outram Road. They always tapped our knees, but most of us had lost our reflexes anyway, and then they would listen to our hearts. Personally, I was so scared at the prospect

125

of going back to that dreaded gaol, that my heart rate must at least have doubled. They generally weighed us, but none of us ever put on any weight, with the rations we were getting, and so most of us remained where we were.

In the bed next to me was Mackay, the Canadian, who told me a lot about fruit growing in the Fraser and Okanagan valleys. It sounded a wonderful life, and the idea appealed to me; perhaps that is why I have spent the last 20 years growing apples and pears.

After my trial, John Wyett and I decided that we would try and build a model of a cruiser-racer, and I drew out the lines of one. In the early days of Changi I had learnt quite a bit about design from the Dutch naval architect I met there, who had also helped me with celestial navigation. The notes that I made on this subject travelled with me on the escape, were confiscated over and over again, and I still have them today.

I suppose we worked on this boat, at odd times, for nearly a year. We obtained the fine teak that we needed for planking by separating the veneers from bits of tea chests. It was a fascinating project and turned out very well, complete with hollow mast and a small anchor, cast from a melted silver coin by an Australian dental friend. Bill Anker reminded me recently that I made a loo and basin from an old porcelain electric light switch, scraping away at it for days. When I met John after the war he told me that the boat had ended up in some war museum in Australia.

Through John I met Russell Braddon and another friend of his, Piddington. Both these men were to become famous in their own ways, Russell Braddon as a writer and broadcaster, and Piddington, with his wife, as an expert in thought transference. Our ward was the first audience before which he performed, using Braddon as his assistant.

I am very glad indeed that John survived all his deprivations. On one of his trips over to England after the war we met for dinner in London, and on a later visit he came down to see us at our home in Sussex.

One of our frequent visitors in the evenings was Tony Chevenix-Trench, who was later to become Headmaster of Eton. It was always a wonderful break in the tedium of our lives to sit outside in a small courtyard, discussing almost every topic under the sun. On other evenings, when we felt there was little likelihood of the guards appearing, we invariably walked together round the perimeter road, just inside the prison walls, trying to get ourselves fit.

When, from the news we heard, it appeared that the Japanese would not be able to hold out for long, there was a general feeling of hope and uncertainty. We wondered what the treatment of prisoners would be when Singapore was reoccupied. Would the Japs hand us over peacefully, or had they other plans?

Later, we occasionally saw B29 American bombers coming overhead, and everyone rushed outside to watch them, but we never saw or heard any bombs being dropped. They must have been flying to more distant missions, but certainly we now began to feel really hopeful. Then we heard of the dropping of the atom bombs on Hiroshima and Nagasaki, but of course we had no idea of the devastation and the terrible consequences that they caused. We only knew that the Americans had taken the war to Japanese territory, and now had the initiative, and we were glad.

I learnt from the prisoners outside the gaol that the Japanese attitude towards us was beginning to change, and that they were becoming less officious, but some held on to their belief that 'Japan Number One; war go on for a hundred years'. Although, theoretically, we were allowed no contact with other officers or the men living outside the prison walls, we had many visitors in the evenings, when guards were thin on the ground. Through these people we kept in touch with the now fast changing conditions of the war.

Wing Commander Atkins was one who regularly came in for a talk, and, unknown to us at the time, just before the end of hostilities he sold his gold watch, which he had retained throughout his captivity, and with the proceeds he managed to obtain some extra food, so that we ex-Outram Road men could hold a celebration before leaving our ward. Bill Anker still has the 'Menu', which I wrote in block letters on paper actually made in the camp, and it bears the signatures of us all. I wish that I had not lost mine. Such was the kindness of so many people during our captivity.

There was no doubt that our guards seemed to be slipping away and there appeared to be few about. Everything happened so quickly, and it was not long before we heard of the final ending of hostilities, and that Singapore had been relieved. The unconditional surrender of Japan was announced on 15th August 1945, and on the 28th August Allied aircraft dropped leaflets over Changi, ordering the Japs to lay down their arms but to continue caring for the prisoners.

We then left our ward inside the gaol and moved out to rejoin friends or units. However, I was still kept in an Australian hospital ward, but now in freedom outside the prison walls. Here I was given a thorough examination by Dr. Bruce Hunt, an Australian, who strongly recommended me to try to get admitted to the Liverpool School of Tropical Medicine, which he said was then the best in the world, and eventually I did just that. Bruce Hunt had been in charge of Tanbaya Hospital, on the Burma end of the railway, where conditions had been so bad.

(ii) The Allies Arrive

On 30th August the first Allies arrived at Changi. They were two doctors and an orderly, who were dropped by parachute, bringing in drugs with them, and on 5th September troops of the 5th Indian Division arrived to reoccupy Changi and take the Japs into custody.

H.M.S. *Sussex* was the first British Naval vessel to enter Singapore Harbour, and the officers and ratings sent up bread and other foods, also new clothes for the few Naval prisoners, which made the rest of us rather envious! Many A.T.S. and W.R.N.S. girls came into the camp, bringing with them bundles of telegram forms for us to fill in and send home. These telegrams were to take a long time to get to their destinations, but the will was there!

It was with enormous relief that I now looked forward to my journey home. My prayers had been answered. Determination, and on many occasions a great deal of luck, had been on my side, and I realized how fortunate I was to be going home to my family. It was sad to think that one third of 18th Division had died as prisoners of war, and my mind went back to that day in October, almost four years ago, when the Division sailed from the Clyde, and I was thinking: 'Would we be the lucky ones to return?' What a dreadful waste of life.

The atomic bombs on Hiroshima and Nagasaki killed approximately 170,000 people, and of the survivors many still suffer from the effects of radiation. Over 102,300 Allied POWs and coolies died at the hands of the Japanese on the Thailand/ Burma railway, many more in appalling conditions in prison camps in the Orient, and more still in overloaded cargo ships taking POWs to work in Japan. Most of these unmarked ships were torpedoed, and the prisoners left to perish in the sea.

The Japanese cruelty was inhuman, and none of the survivors of captivity will ever forget the beatings, kickings, tortures and suffering that were inflicted on them. For these survivors the memory of their sufferings will remain with them for the rest of their lives, and indeed many POWs have suffered physically as well as mentally ever since, if they have not already died prematurely as a result of it all. How many more Allied POWs would have suffered and died, had not those two atomic bombs been dropped?

Having been confined within the walls of Changi Gaol I did not realise at the time, but have learnt since, that POWs were made to dig large trenches—mass graves for themselves. Had an Allied landing on Japan taken place, there would have been a total massacre of all surviving prisoners-of-war and civilian internees, including women and children, not just at Changi, but in all Japanese internment camps throughout the Far East. Instructions to commandants were that no traces should remain.

There was, in fact, a planned landing. General MacArthur and Admiral Nimitz were to land in Japan in November 1945, with a further landing in March 1946, and for this they had allowed 1,000,000 casualties (not deaths). The Japanese, on their part, were prepared to accept the loss of 10,000,000 men in opposing such a landing.

Liberated POWs included 37,500 British, 14,400 Australian,

16,912 American, plus those of the Indian Army and Dutch forces. Had those atomic bombs not fallen, I calculate that instead of 170,000 deaths, there could well have been several million.

The Japanese advance through to India was finally stopped in 1944 by the British and Indians, on the borders of Burma and India. The inscription on the Kohima Memorial, in this remote mountainous area, says it all:

> 'When you go home
> Tell them of us and say
> For your tomorrow
> We gave our today.'

The futility of war! As the Bishop of Singapore said, we should forgive but not forget. Indeed, we can't forget.

(iii) Journey Home

I was one of the first to leave Changi, as I was being evacuated by hospital ship. It seemed strange to be taken away from the camp and actually to know where we were going! On the way down to the docks we passed parties of Japanese prisoners filling in trenches and generally tidying up, but it gave me no particular pleasure to witness their humiliation. As far as I remember, we were a fairly quiet group in the truck, as perhaps we had not yet taken in the full meaning of our changed circumstances.

We soon arrived at the docks and embarked on an old Henderson Line ship, the *Amarapura*, which had been converted for hospital work. I just could not believe the cleanliness and apparent feeling of space, and everywhere the friendly, smiling faces of the crew and nursing staff in their sparkling white uniforms. White was a colour that had been entirely lacking in our lives for so long; the only time I remembered seeing anything really white was when the Italian submarine personnel were brought into Changi, wearing white tropical kit.

We had baths or showers and were then put to bed in loaned pyjamas and crisp, clean sheets, and generally thoroughly spoilt. It was wonderful to talk to new people from the outside world, who could tell us so much of what we had missed. The nurses and medical staff never seemed to be rushed, and always made time to talk to us, which was what we wanted more than anything else. There was certainly no medical reason for us to be in bed, although we revelled in the luxury of it for a time.

Before we sailed Lady Louis Mountbatten visited us in our hospital bay. She had obviously been exceedingly well briefed, as she knew I had been in Outram Road Gaol, and told me that the Japanese NCO, 'The Cat', who had been our warder, was himself now in one of our cells. She really was most charming, putting us completely at ease, and we all greatly appreciated her visit, especially as her time must have been so fully occupied. Her husband, being the Supreme Commander of the Allied Forces, South-East Asia, had personally accepted the surrender of the Japanese forces in Singapore. She noticed my photograph of Roger and a friend of his, Penny Knowles, which was on my bedside table, and said what attractive children they were. It was a pity I didn't know at the time that Penny was her sister's godchild.

During our conversation Lady Mountbatten said that I really ought to write a book about our escape and the subsequent events after recapture. However, I explained to her why I had no wish to do this; if I kept to the truth, it would be too distressing for the wives and relatives of those who had died in such terrible circumstances, and if I did not keep to the truth, there would be no point in writing it.

However, now that 38 years have elapsed I have been persuaded to record my story, with certain harrowing omissions, as our experiences were unique in the history of escape attempts in South-East Asia.

After leaving Singapore we persuaded the nursing staff to allow us to get up from our beds and, as we sailed north through the Straits of Malacca and into the Indian Ocean, we spent much of our time on deck, just leaning against the rails, talking and watching the sunsets at dusk and the moonglade in the evening. It was hard to believe that we were at last going in the right direction, surrounded by so much kindness and beauty. Our ship had a very low cruising speed and, even with all this beauty around us, we began to long impatiently for the next stage of our journey.

As we approached the dockside at Madras we could see a

large reception party and a military band playing. There were many Red Cross ambulances also awaiting our arrival and, as we were the first hospital ship, it was thought appropriate that some of us should be returned to bed and carried off by stretcher! Thus I disembarked and was taken, with others, to the hospital train which was standing nearby.

On this train the nursing sisters again insisted on our taking to our bunks. We travelled through the night, and next day, on arrival at Bangalore, ambulances met us and took us to a huge military hospital just outside the town.

The time must have been the end of September or early October 1945. The first thing I did, on arrival at this hospital, was to cable Lindsay to let her know I was safe and well in India, and she immediately cabled back, letting me know that they too were well and overjoyed at receiving my message. She also transferred some money to me in Bangalore.

Although Lindsay had received no further postcards from me after my first one as a prisoner, she was sent a strange message a few months before the end of the war. It was picked up by Signals in Reading, addressed to: 'Walker, Colwyn Bay'; Walker was her maiden name. The message simply said: 'Tell Lindsay Jim O.K.'. It has always been a mystery as to how this signal was received. I know that at one time some Australians were allowed to send a radio message home, and I can only think that it may have been one of these kind people, with no family of his own, who, knowing that my position was so much worse than most others, decided to do this. When one has been at close quarters for so long, there is very little that one doesn't know about each other's families and where they live. Who-ever did this was very thoughtful in not mentioning me by name, as the message might have been spotted and destroyed.

We had a wonderful time in Bangalore, going down into the town most days. During our voyage on the hospital ship I had been lucky enough to meet and become friendly with someone called Wichers; I am not sure from which regiment he came, but he had a marvellous sense of humour and we laughed a lot. He knew a serving officer stationed in Banga-lore, Col. Scott, and his charming wife, who were extremely hospitable and asked me along, with Wichers, to their home. They also took us to lunch at the Bangalore Cricket Club.

I wanted to take home to Lindsay a gold sari, from which to have an evening dress made. Mrs. Scott came with me to help barter for this, and I finally spent all the money that Lindsay had cabled to me on this beautiful sari! However, by now we had been given a certain amount of army pay, so I was not completely penniless.

Whilst in Bangalore, I received a visit from Daryl Morgan, who was stationed there and must have seen my name on the list of prisoners coming through. He was the son of a North Wales solicitor whom I knew quite well at home. I was given leave to stay away from the hospital for one night, and Daryl gave a tremendous party for me, and put me up in his mess.

Although I was moving about fairly freely, the medical authorities decided that it would be unwise for me to leave hospital and return to England before Christmas, and so I wrote to Lindsay to this effect. However, I then received a letter from her, telling me that she had had a minor car accident and had broken her nose. This had happened the day she received my cable saying that I was safe, and while on her way to tell my mother the news, she ran into a lamp-post! This in itself was not serious, but I immediately went to see the Brigadier commanding the hospital and told him of Lindsay's accident, and that it was the first letter I had received for so long. I asked him if I could be allowed to fly home, on compassionate grounds!

As usual, we went down into Bangalore for the rest of the day, returning to the hospital at about nine o'clock in the evening. As I entered my ward I was greeted by the night sister, who said: 'Thank God you have come back! You are being discharged at seven o'clock tomorrow morning'. With that, she gave me a rail warrant to take me from Bangalore to Poona, but had no other documents for me.

So, early next morning, I was taken to Bangalore Station, whence I set off on my own, with no responsibility for any troops and with very little idea as to how I should reach home; not that this worried me very much. In my compartment I fell in with an American, who was also travelling up to Poona. He was well stocked with canned and other foods, which he shared with me in the train.

At Poona I saw the Adjutant of the RAF and told him that I was an ex-prisoner of war, travelling home on compassionate grounds, and was there anything he could do to help? He got me on to a plane leaving within the hour for Karachi.

On arrival in Karachi I again told my sob story to the Adjutant. He was horrified to find that I had no clothes, apart from my khaki shirt, shorts and stockings that had been issued to me on the hospital ship, and some tropical kit I had bought in Bangalore, so he produced a battle-dress for me, together with a mosquito net. I had never seen a battle-dress quite like this one, as it was made for paratroopers, and seemed to have unlimited washleather-lined pockets throughout, which were of little use to me. He was able to put me on a plane the following day for Lydda, near Jerusalem.

At Lydda I again tried to get a flight, but was told very emphatically that I must stay here for a period of at least 48 hours' acclimatization. To fill in the time I went by taxi to Tel Aviv with two medical officers, but returned to the camp after lunch as these two were intent on a pretty heavy drinking session, which I knew could do me no good, not yet being properly accustomed to food, let alone drink. This was the last day on which military personnel were allowed into Tel Aviv without carrying side arms. Whilst in Lydda I swapped my mosquito net with an Arab for a basket of oranges, only to find on arrival home that neither Lindsay nor Roger were particularly keen on oranges; but the basket has been used ever since for carrying logs!

After my 48 hours in Lydda I set off on the final stage of my journey, flying in the belly of a Liberator bomber. We were on rather uncomfortable benches in the bomb-racks of the plane, and I have never been so cold in my life! In the cold dawn we landed in North Africa, at Castel Benito or Idris Air Base, and, after a good breakfast and refuelling of the aircraft, we took off again, landing that same evening at Bourne Aerodrome in Cambridgeshire.

I was on English soil! The Customs officials asked me whether I had anything to declare, and tried to decide what they should charge me for the gold sari but, when they realized that I had no papers and was an ex-POW, they sent me on my way.

The authorities at Bourne were very thoughtful, saying that if I lived within 50 miles they would run me home for the night, and pick me up in the morning in time to get a train to London. As 18th Division was basically an East Anglian Division they assumed, presumably, that I lived nearby.

I rang through to Lindsay in Wales. She could hardly believe it, having only just received my letter, telling her it was unlikely that I should be home for Christmas! She begged to come down to meet me in London next day, but I persuaded her not to come, as I didn't know how long my debriefing would take, and in any case I intended to be in Wales by the evening.

The amazing thing about my journey home was the fact that I had no papers whatsoever, identity or medical. I was asked for them on arrival at each airfield, but on every occasion my word was accepted and I was allowed to continue my journey.

The following morning I went by train from Cambridge to London and reported to the War Office. I was interviewed by people in various departments, all of whom seemed interested in the fact that I had travelled home from Bangalore to London with no identity papers or other documents. The medical authorities, to whom I was then passed, were equally incredulous. After answering all their questions, they gave me lunch and then telephoned Euston Station to find the time of the next train to North Wales, and, somewhat unnecessarily, reserved a whole compartment for me!

I was driven to the station with my few possessions, which included the basket of oranges and gold sari, which I had bought for Lindsay. I think my driver must have felt rather foolish carrying the oranges to the train for me!

To my astonishment, my sister Beth happened to be travelling up on the same train! She was returning from duty in Germany, where she had nursed for three months at Belsen Camp as part of the first contingent of VAD to enter the camp, and was due for leave before being posted to India and Assam, still as a VAD. She spotted me waiting to board the train, but was completely taken aback, as she too thought I was not returning until after Christmas, and in any case, I now looked rather different, having no glasses and being fat in the face through beri-beri.

Beth had just met another officer travelling up to Wales, so naturally they both joined me in my compartment, as did a Norwegian who was returning home from some expedition. Beth tells me that I talked non-stop for most of the journey. Having thus got it out of my system, I was then very reluctant to speak of my experiences for many years to come, which I believe was a common feature of many returning Japanese POWs.

When the train eventually pulled out of Chester Station I felt I was on home ground. The line runs alongside the Dee Estuary until the Point of Ayr, and from there onwards I should be within sight of the sea until reaching home. As we passed Llandulas, I looked up to see my preparatory school, Arnold House, on the side of the hill, but sadly its grounds had been developed before the war and it was no longer a school.

Dusk was falling, but it made no difference as I knew the country so well and within a quarter of an hour we would reach Colwyn Bay.

As I stepped from the train, I just could not believe my eyes when I saw Lindsay waiting for me on the platform. No words can express our happiness.

We took Beth home and I saw my mother briefly, before driving on to Lindsay's parents' home, where she and Roger had been living during the war. We were anxious to get back to Roger as Lindsay had told me that he was trying hard to stay awake to see me. We went straight upstairs to his room and found him almost asleep, but without hesitation or reserve he flung his arms round my neck, and said: 'Oh Daddy, you have changed!' This spontaneity was entirely due to Lindsay's forethought in keeping my photograph beside his bed, and talking to him about me before he went to sleep.

Now we were all together again. This was the moment towards which I had been striving for nearly four years, and without this goal I really do not think I should have survived. What an incredibly lucky man I was.

APPENDICES

(i) Roberts Hospital, Changi

THE MAIN POW HOSPITAL was opened, under Lt.-Col. F. H. A. Davidson, I.M.S., in Roberts Barracks on 24th February 1942, within one week of our being concentrated in Changi. 550 beds had been made ready for patients in extremely cramped quarters. These were barrack rooms, each having been designed for 40 fit soldiers, and were therefore dreadfully overcrowded with 140 wounded patients in each room.

Roberts Barracks was one of the six Areas that constituted the POW Camp, Changi, and in 1938 had been occupied by the East Surreys and a Searchlight Regiment. It was in the centre of the camp, and could easily be identified from anywhere in the Camp Area because of the height of the famous 'Changi Tree'. Incidentally, the top of the tree had been removed during hostilities, as it would have proved such a landmark for the enemy.

On the opening of Roberts Hospital all subsidiary hospitals were closed, with the exception of the one which was being established by the Australians at Selarang Barracks. The gross overcrowding, the limited water supply, the absence of artificial lighting, the lack of proper means of sewage disposal and the shortage of stores and equipment, in conjunction with a high admittance rate before organization was complete, all presented enormous difficulties in the early days and made nursing in the dark a nightmare for both patients and staff alike. By 28th February, Roberts Hospital housed 1,033 cases, and at one time the Hospital Area contained a population equivalent to 84,000 to the square mile. There were no nurses, so officers had to do the nursing themselves, which

137

they did very successfully until they themselves contracted diseases.

Lt.-Col. L. G. Pearson, I.M.S., took over command from Lt.-Col. Davidson on 25th February, and was succeeded three days later by Lt.-Col. J. W. Craven, R.A.M.C., who ran the hospital for eight months before handing over command, at his own request, on 27th October to Lt.-Col. J. C. Collins, R.A.M.C., 36 Field Ambulance.

Roberts Hospital enjoyed the privileges of an independent Area, but was dependent on 18th Division for R.E. work, maintenance and Courts Martial. I came to be involved with the hospital as Wilkie had taken over as C.R.E. 18th Division about two to three days before the capitulation, when Col. Sydenham, our previous C.R.E., had left with an official party of senior and some junior officers, and Wilkie delegated the Divisional sapper work at the hospital to me.

It was absorbing work for the 14 months I remained in Changi, and I was grateful for the fact that I could contribute in some small way towards improving the facilities at the hospital, and also for being associated with those medical officers and orderlies whose selfless and untiring efforts achieved so much.

They started a hospital with nothing but the equipment they were able to bring out from the Singapore hospitals, with very limited transport. In the official medical report they thank all those who were responsible for collecting and transporting to Changi anything which could help in the establishment of a hospital, so sorely needed. Beds, operating theatre equipment, instruments and a shadowless light arrived, also a mobile autoclave for sterilization; but as yet we had no electricity, except a portable generator which supplied light for the operating theatre. We managed to rig up a steam pipe from the cookhouse to the autoclave, which was better than nothing, but we could not maintain a pressure that would ensure reliable sterilization. However, on 15th August 1942, the IJA made electricity available, and so one problem, at least, was overcome.

In a few cases, where the drainage was intact, it was possible to improvise a flushing system from storm water. Sometimes sea water was carted up and used for flushing, but this was too demanding on labour, and eventually we managed to get a water-borne sewage system operating.

The Australian Hospital, which had been based at Selarang Barracks, was very soon ordered by the IJA to move to Roberts Hospital and make one large unit, and this move began on 8th March 1942. 4,000 men were crowded into an area designed for 750, and in this area were located all latrines and refuse pits. Later, I was asked to take over the R.E. maintenance for this part of the hospital as well, and by so doing I made many good Australian friends, among them two dentists, John Searby and John Ross. John Searby's sister and her daughter came to stay with us after the war.

I think it is a great credit to all the medical personnel that they were able to accept 39,416 admissions in the first 12 months, a ratio of 944.12 per thousand average strength. I have since heard that this was the greatest number of patients for any hospital in the world at that time. These patients had dysentery, diphtheria, beri-beri and malaria, but by far the greater percentage were dysentery cases. Deaths numbered 548 in that first year.

Distilled water was produced from a still, fed by steam from the hospital cookhouse, and for intravenous injections rain was collected and put through the autoclave before use.

The barrack kitchen attached to the hospital blocks had been badly damaged by bomb-blast, and it was not until April 1942 that the Royal Engineers were able to effect sufficient repairs for it to be used efficiently. In the meantime, a cookhouse for patients operated in a temporary wooden hut on a concrete floor.

Within a few days of the opening of the hospital, an operating theatre was in action, using equipment transferred from the Singapore hospitals, and the first operation took place on 2nd March. Water was supplied by hand carriage, and we were able to supply, almost immediately, electricity from a small diesel generator.

There were never enough sheets or pillowcases, and laundry facilities for them were almost nil. Washing the linen in the sea had been tried at first, but it never looked really clean, and men often had to use pillows without cases.

As the buildings had been used previously as barrack blocks, all the wards were alive with bed bugs. These were difficult to eradicate, as there were few blow lamps and no fuel for them. Before hostilities, time had been allowed to the troops each week for de-bugging the tubular iron bedsteads by means of a hot blow lamp.

By May 1942 we had made a fly-proof 'Clean Theatre', with all openings covered with wire gauze, and with a special outlet for steam. This was immediately brought into use by the surgeons, and no unhealed wound was admitted to this theatre. It was staffed by the R.A.M.C., but was used by Australian surgeons for three days a week, with the help of R.A.M.C. personnel.

Several attempts were made at producing artificial legs, but none were really satisfactory. However, in May 1942, following a request from Col. Julian Taylor (lately Consulting Surgeon Malaya Command), Capt. R. Bradley, R.A., 88 Field Regiment, was appointed to take charge of an artificial limb factory. He was an engineer in peacetime, and was at once able to apply himself to the problem of producing stable, mobile limbs. In the end, nearly 40 satisfactory artificial legs were produced, and Major Walsh, R.I.A.O.C., made nine artificial arms.

The main materials available were aluminium fan blades, copper wire for rivets, and steel from the cupboards used in the barrack blocks, and corsets were made from old fire hose, laced with string. All the buckets had to be made to fit individual stumps after amputation and, as there was no plaster-of-Paris to make moulds, wooden carvings were made in the likeness of each stump; I well remember Capt. Cook, 5th Suffolk Regiment, carving away at hunks of teak or rubber wood.

These caring doctors, with their devoted helpers and orderlies, were to my mind the real heroes of our captivity. Thankfully, Col. Julian Taylor was not taken to Formosa (Taiwan) with all the other senior officers in August 1942 and was thus able to continue with his wonderful work at the hospital for the rest of the war. I believe he was the only senior officer to remain in Changi, apart from Gen. Sir Lewis Heath, GOC 3rd Indian Corps.

When Lt.-Col. Collins took over command of the hospital in October 1942 the sanitation of the Area was well established. Flush system was working in the wards, and bore-hole latrines and Otway pits were scattered throughout the Area. The water supply, however, was still irregular.

That autumn a large batch of POWs arrived from Java, which created a sharp rise in dysentery admissions, and diphtheria then reached its peak. Diphtheria was endemic among the native population of Singapore, and sporadic cases had appeared both in Changi and in the working camps in Singapore, from March to June 1942, but it increased to epidemic numbers in August and September. The tragedy of the epidemic was the high death rate, but the numbers and mortality among Australian troops was much lower than that of the British. The Australians had better spacing in their quarters, and a considerably higher age incidence, 30 years as compared with 24 years for 18th Division. Whether this age difference was significant is debatable.

In February 1943, as a result of parties leaving Changi for unknown destinations, the population of Changi was down to 28,000, of whom 7,000 were Dutch. These smaller numbers did much to alleviate overcrowding.

In April 1943 parties leaving Changi recommenced, and 7,000 Australian and British left, followed by an additional 3,000. These were known as 'F' and 'H' Forces, but nothing was known of their intended destination, the authorities having been told they would be going to good camps, where the Japanese would be better able to care for them and rations would be good.

Rumours of their fate eventually trickled through to Changi, but misgivings arose when a further party of 230 medical officers and men were hastily called for in June.

As I went to Thailand with 'F' Force, I no longer had any connection with Roberts Hospital, until I returned months later as a very sick patient. By this time the hospital had been moved to Selarang Barracks, on orders from the

IJA. This movement was completed by 27th August 1943, and the reason for it was that the Japanese wanted to convert part of Changi into an aerodrome, utilizing the POW labour which was immediately to hand.

The return of 'F' Force and, to a lesser extent, 'H' Force, threw another tremendous burden on the hospital, as these men were in an advanced state of malnutrition and suffering from dysentery, for which the hospital now had no cure, as stocks of Emetine had been completely exhausted. This was another instance of Japanese incompetence or indifference. At Highlands Estate, near Klang, there was an enormous acreage planted with *Cephaelis Ipecacuanha*, the official source of Ipecacuanha B.P., which could have supplied all the requirements of Emetine, but the Japs scarcely exploited it until the end of the war. Cases of beri-beri again rose to alarming proportions and malaria once more became a serious threat. Besides these diseases, men with tropical ulcers and pellagra returned in massive numbers.

The incidence of diphtheria also reappeared and strangely enough it was again higher in 18th Division, with its younger average age. The Annual Medical Report, POW Camp Changi, Part 2 states that malaria was no longer a problem until the return of 'F' Force in December 1943, although the precarious position as regards control was always present. However, as soon as 'F' Force returned, the position at once worsened, and a survey showed that 80-90% of the remnants of the Force were probably infected and, with relapses, 1,000 cases monthly were expected. Towards the end of 1944, malaria became the most important problem in the camp, and even the benign tertian variety was a serious factor in the health of 'F' Force. This was not because of the virulence of the parasite, but because of the undernourished state of the Force.

During the last ten days of December 1943 the remnants of this pitiful party returned to Changi. 3,000 men had died of illness, malnutrition and overwork on the railway and, of the 1,000 men who had been left behind in Burma and Thailand, many more must also have died.

It shows the utter disaster of 'F' Force that within six months over half the Force had died and that, from those who were brought back to Changi, the Japanese medical authorities could find only 125 men fit enough even for light duties. This was during an inspection, six weeks after their return, to try and find more labour for the continued construction of the aerodrome. They were completely relentless in their search for labour.

(ii) MBE Citation

CITATION, LONDON GAZETTE, 11.2.49
M.B.E.

Lieutenant James Bottomley Bradley (155989),
Corps of Royal Engineers

Lieutenant Bradley was one of a party of eight officers, one NCO and a Chittagong native, who escaped from a prisoner of war camp in Thailand, knowing full well the extreme penalties exacted by the Japanese, if recaptured.

Their object was to reach the British lines and let the world know of the terrible conditions under which the Japanese forced British and Imperial prisoners of war to work in the building of the Burma/Thailand railway. In this way they hoped to ameliorate the conditions prevailing in the camps along the railway, where a large percentage of the prisoners were ill and many had died of disease, malnutrition, and allied complaints.

After eight weeks of extreme hardships and privations in cutting their way through the dense jungle — the last three weeks they lived on water only — they reached the Tavoy coast. Five of the party were unable to survive the terrible hardships endured during this journey.

Lieutenant Bradley and the other survivors of the party, when almost in sight of their goal, were recaptured through the treachery of a Burman. During his trial by the Japanese, through his fortitude and bearing, he upheld the finest traditions of the British Army. He was one of the few who escaped the extreme penalty of death, which was the usual sentence for having escaped, and was sentenced to eight years penal servitude.

(iii) Post-war Personalia

Nur Mahommed: After the war Bill Anker was instrumental in getting Nur Mahommed a grant of land in Malaya, and a permanent pension. When he joined the escape party, Wilkie had promised that he would do what he could to see that Nur Mahommed received some tangible recognition for his services, if he should survive the escape attempt. Bill Anker, therefore, approached Lord Louis Mountbatten, who agreed to honour this promise.

Bill Anker: By the end of the war Bill was amazingly fit. He was a regular soldier, and when someone with experience was required to restart the working of Singapore Docks, Bill volunteered. He remained in Malaya for several years, and I believe that at one time he had a work force of many thousands under him. His future wife, Joan, flew out there to marry him, and they had two daughters.

Ian Moffat: Ian has worked for the same company in South America since April 1946, and is in good health. He married in 1948 and has three sons, one daughter and three grand-daughters.

Guy Machado: Guy survived the war and went back to his profession of teaching, in Malaya. I don't think that he ever became really fit again, and during the last years of his life he was plagued by the memory of the horrors of the escape. He died in 1957, at the age of 50, having turned to religion for comfort.

I fulfilled the promise that I had made to myself in Outram Road, which was that I would farm, if I survived the war, and I therefore went, as a pupil, on a farm in Wiltshire. For several years I spent much time in and out of hospital, but eventually made a complete recovery, and am now very fit again.

For 13 years I ran a farm belonging to friends at Loxwood in Sussex. However, in 1960 I purchased my own fruit farm, also in Sussex, together with a beautiful timbered farmhouse, which we renovated. We loved that house, but in 1977 we sold it and, although I still grow apples, it is on a much smaller scale, and on land adjoining Roger's house, and owned by him.

Roger followed me to the same house at Oundle and the same college at Cambridge, and he is now married and lives not far from us.

We had a wonderful and extremely happy life, until Lindsay became seriously ill. This incurable illness lasted for six years, but at least I was able to look after her at home until she died in 1969.

Later, I married again, Lindy, the daughter of our neighbouring fruit grower, and much younger than I. We have a son, Timothy, nine, and a daughter, Sarah, six, and once again I lead a very happy and full life. I am indeed lucky to have had two such wonderful marriages, and our children are a great joy, especially as I missed such a large part of Roger's childhood.